CW00322320

'There have been a number of [...]
ministry when I have had [...]
cancer. Although everyone w[...]
miraculous healing, I know [...]
grace while pressing on throu~~~ ~~~ ~~~ just as inspiring. This is
a great story that fits right into this category. Thank you, Matt,
for sharing it, and I pray that it will be an encouragement to
many.'
*Dr Hugh Osgood, president of Churches in Communities
International*

'Matt, thank you for writing your breath-taking journey in this
way. A wonderful reminder of God's peace and presence during
the challenging times. So helpfully written, filled with heartache
and buckets of hope.'
*Rev Cris Rogers, author, chair of the Spring Harvest Planning Group,
rector of All Hallows Bow, London*

'Matt tells the moving story of his life in Africa, his move to the
UK and then how his young family went through the turmoil of
the onset of cancer, and their subsequent deliverances. It is a
great account of faith triumphing over adversity – one with
which I can so identify because of my life in Africa, and losing
my first wife through cancer. May all who read it be edified and
blessed!'
*Patrick Johnstone, international speaker and author emeritus
Operation World (Zondervan)*

'Here is a memoir that will touch your heart when following
Matt through his unusual childhood in Zimbabwe, his journey
into faith and his desperate move to the UK. God has been with
him, putting him in the right place, the right job and with the
right people around him to help him cope with a devastating
diagnosis of Stage Four cancer. This is not a classic "feel-good"
book – it is real and gritty, yet reveals God's great love and

faithfulness throughout Matt's joyous times as well as through great grief, including unpleasant and traumatic treatment.'
Angela Hobday, consultant clinical psychologist (retired)

'Authentic and inspiring! Matt McChlery's book *Standing in the Storm* captivates the reader in its gripping realness. He is able to take you on the journey through diagnosis, fear, pain, brokenness, hope and faith. And through his own brave documenting of his experiences of cancer you feel inspired to live, to laugh, to love and to be thankful for the privileges of life and even of growing old. Through his story you feel the pull to hope and to believe, whatever your own battles are. Having met Matt years ago at university, and having seen some of his journey with God over the years, I applaud this book as one that tells a story of a David against a Goliath, and we know who wins.

'Books like these cost so much to write in ways those who have never dealt with a dread disease cannot know, but I am grateful that he has written it and it will forever stand as a pillar of hope and truth for many, a memorial stone to the kindness of God and a beacon of light in the darkness for those who know the pain of suffering.

'I believe it will pour courage into many!'
Denise Padayachee, author, founder of Wells Training and Missions, Cape Town

'What do you do when the bad news seems to crush all the good news, and a combination of life and death experiences throws you into a tailspin? Matt's book, *Standing in the Storm*, is vulnerable yet hopeful and will give you a renewed, robust confidence in Jesus, no matter what struggle is staring you down.'
Tommy Deuschle, pastor, Celebrate International Church

'Cancer isn't convenient. It disrupts lives and challenges our view of ourselves and our world. For the Christian, its shocking diagnosis also brings into question what we think we know of God. All this was Matt's experience, which he relates with disarming honesty in this book. He already knew of God as Saviour and rescuer through his conversion in his native Zimbabwe, but now had to ask: could God be his healer, too?

'I read *Standing in the Storm* in two sittings, unable to put it down. The fascinating descriptions of his early life in African culture provide a great backdrop to what was waiting for him in Britain: a new teaching career, a wife and... non-Hodgkin lymphoma. Extracts from his blog/journal, written at the time, ensure that this is no sanitised, after-the-event story but a pulling-no-punches account of a journey he didn't want to make. Through it all, hope shines through the despair and pain – a hope based on God, the only One who can keep us standing in the storm.'

Jane Walters, author, vice-chair of ACW and leader of Brecks, Fens and Pens writing group

Standing in the Storm

Living with Faith and Cancer

Matt McChlery

instant
ap☐stle

First published in Great Britain in 2022

Instant Apostle
104 The Drive
Rickmansworth
Herts
WD3 4DU

British Library Cataloguing-in-Publication Data

A catalogue record for this book is available from the British Library.

This book and all other Instant Apostle books are available from Instant Apostle:

Website: www.instantapostle.com

Email: info@instantapostle.com

ISBN 978-1-912726-53-0

Printed in Great Britain.

For my amazing children
Katrina, Lara and Elijah

Contents

Foreword
Paul Nyamuda

A couple of years ago I preached on the technology of spiritual strength. In this series, I attempted to articulate some of the keys to strengthening ourselves in God. *Standing in the Storm* is an account of how Matt used one of these keys; a journey to a place of absolute dependence on God, and making Him his only anchor. I really love the way in which Matt writes. Once I started reading it, I found this book very difficult to put down. It's quite an art, to be able to take you on such an emotional journey that edifies you spiritually while simultaneously educating you about the dynamics around cancer.

I believe this is a book about attitude, perspective and choices. Through reading it I have been reminded of how we have the power to choose our attitude and perspective. I am grateful for Matt's vulnerability and transparency, which will inspire any parent or spouse. The book is also relevant for leaders, and one of my favourite quotes is, 'Sharing something personal and painful clothed in humility and vulnerability was part of the package for an authentic leader, not a sign of weakness.' Matt described what he went through as a leader who had to leave a legacy through effective delegation. He encourages us as leaders to do the same, whether we are ill or not. He says, 'Leaders should not only focus on the here and now but also on the future. This includes a future without them. Good leaders lead in the here and now. Excellent leaders lead with the future in mind.' In his book, Matt brilliantly communicates the biblical worldview in a way that models how God applies to all aspects of life.

I also appreciate how Matt took the time to journal and blog about his experiences as his writing candidly paints a vivid picture of what people and their families go through after a diagnosis of critical illness. Reading *Standing in the Storm* will give you a deeper appreciation of the pain and emotional struggles cancer patients and their families go through. Matt takes us through the psychological journey one embarks on when facing death; how it affects our view of use of time and changes our bad habits, such as procrastination.

This piece of literature inspires us to view life from the perspective of eternity, re-evaluating our values and priorities. It is an apt reminder of how Matt's experiences can happen to anyone. Matt is one of the most God-fearing, caring, gracious and tender people I know, so yes, bad things happen to good people. Reading this book helps you even if you are not facing critical illness. It can be applied to all kinds of challenges we face as human beings.

Finally, deeply embedded in *Standing in the Storm* are timeless values: patience, humility, empathy, faith, passion, focus, relinquishment and many others. Matt shows us how to turn pain into progress and tragedy into triumph. I trust that you will allow this wonderful book to inform and edify you as I have allowed it to do to me.

Paul Nyamuda
Speaker, author, executive coach and senior pastor of Go Church, Johannesburg

Introduction

We have this hope as an anchor for the soul, firm and
secure.
(Hebrews 6:19)

There is an old story about two guys.[1] They were both in
need of a house. They didn't get on their smartphones and
start searching on the housing sales websites to see what
was on the market. (This story was told well before
smartphones were invented, or estate agents for that
matter.) No. Instead, they both set about building their
own houses in the same town that ran alongside a lovely,
scenic river.

One guy, let's call him Ed, decided that he would build
steadily and carefully. He would find out what the best
building materials were, as well as the techniques he
would need to learn in order to build a safe house that
would not only look good, but would also do the desired
job of providing shelter by standing up to the elements.
He found a solid piece of rocky ground where he dug
strong foundations that were deep enough to hold his

---

[1] Based on Matthew 7:24-27.

house firmly. Sure, this would take time and effort and would probably be costly, but the end result would be worth it.

The other guy, whom we will call Ted, was only interested in the quick fix. He did a bodge-job and cobbled together any old bits and pieces. He wasn't terribly concerned about how to build his house correctly so did not learn any techniques or house-building skills. He found a patch of sandy ground and didn't bother with underpinning or foundations. He just grabbed a hammer and some nails, and before you knew it he had constructed a house. It actually looked quite good and the shelves he had put up were surprisingly straight. He had hooked up a line from the electricity cable outside, so he even had quite a few home comforts.

Both Ed and Ted were very happy with their finished houses.

A few months after they had finished building, a huge storm came. The thunder was so loud that it shook the ground, and the lightning flashed and cracked so fiercely that both Ed and Ted were afraid and took shelter in their homes. The wind beat against the houses. Hailstones hammered down on the roofs. There was so much rain that the river flooded, and no matter how many sandbags they piled up against their doors, the floodwaters swept in.

Once the storm had passed and things had settled a little, the residents of the town emerged to see what the extent of the damage was.

Ed's house had been flooded. He would have to replace the carpets and probably needed to replaster the walls on the ground floor. But all in all, his house was still standing, and he had been protected from the worst of the storm's assault.

Sadly, Ted was not as fortunate. His house was no longer standing. In fact, in the middle of the storm it had been completely destroyed and Ted had been swept away by the flood surge. He was found by a rescue boat, struggling to stay afloat amid the debris and swirling currents he had suddenly found himself in. But his house was gone.

This story is a metaphor for how we choose to build and live our lives.

Ed built wisely, taking the time to learn and to use good-quality materials as well as to build the very important foundations upon which the rest of the house stood. Unlike Ted's, his house was able to weather the storms of life and continued to stand even after it had taken a battering.

This book is my story.

Like Ed and Ted's houses, my life has been through many storms. However, there is one storm in particular that I want to tell you about, because if it hadn't been for my firm and secure foundation based on a relationship with Jesus, I wouldn't have been able to weather that storm and would have certainly been swept away.

In early 2016 I was diagnosed with Stage Four non-Hodgkin lymphoma, a form of cancer. I was thirty-six years old.

Through a very turbulent year when the storms of life were raging at their strongest, I experienced joy and success within the suffering, as well as seeing God move in some amazing ways.

I journaled these experiences in a blog I was writing at the time – partly as a way of helping me to process things, as well as a way of keeping concerned friends and family informed. It was also my prayer that God would use my experiences to inspire and bring hope to others. This is how the book you now have in your hands came into being.

In the early days of the blog, it became obvious that this was also a way in which I could share my faith in Jesus with others. Literally hundreds of thousands of people from around the world started reading and following it – some I knew and many more I did not. In fact, this led to me becoming a finalist in the national Premier Digital Awards 2016, in the 'Most Inspiring Leadership Blog' category.

For me, faith and lifestyle cannot be separated. So even in the darkest part of my life, in the middle of the mess and suffering, Jesus was there, holding my hand and giving me the strength I needed to simply stand in the storm.

One thing I learned during this experience is that there are literally hundreds of types of cancer. Along with that, there are many different kinds of treatments and different combinations of chemotherapy. I can only speak from the experience I had, about the particular cancer and type of chemotherapy I went through. If you are reading this book because you or someone you know has cancer, please bear in mind that your experience will invariably be different from mine. However, I have received many responses and comments on my blog from different people saying that the insight given has been helpful to them as a cancer sufferer as well as to those seeking a better understanding of what a loved one is going through.

The aim of this book is not to depress you. It is to show you that even in the darkest moments, God is with you. I hope it inspires you and gives you a fresh perspective on faith in Jesus and on life – life that is worth living!

Matt McChlery

1
Colouring Within the Lines

Leather shoes could be heard slapping the polished concrete of the hospital floor as the doctor came sprinting down the corridor. He had been out for dinner that evening when the call came that he should come quickly. Still in suit and tie, he rushed through the hospital to the maternity unit. Finding my mother in the last throes of labour, he managed to swing his tie over his shoulder just in time to catch me as I made my entrance into the world. At least, that's how the story goes, according to my mother.

It's one of those stories that gets brought up at family barbecues or at weddings. The sort that make me smile politely yet leaves me feeling I can't quite contribute, as I can't remember any part of it. So I smile and nod, yet quietly ponder, 'Did it really happen like that?' But who am I to question the fond stories my mother tells? It is the story of my birth. My first breath. The beginning of an amazing adventure.

The world I was born into was an uncertain and changing one. The year was 1979 and there was a civil war raging in the country of my birth, Zimbabwe.

Southern Rhodesia was established as a British colony in the south of Africa in the 1920s after previously being purchased by the British South African Company who were prospecting for gold. In 1965, the white minority government declared independence from the British. After this, the country was known as Rhodesia. The African majority strongly objected to this arrangement and so a brutal fifteen-year civil war ensued.

The year of my birth saw an end to white minority rule as a new government was created and the country renamed Zimbabwe-Rhodesia. However, this did not last long as it failed to receive international recognition.

It wasn't until 1980, when the war ended and new elections were held under British and Commonwealth supervision, that the new nation of Zimbabwe was born.

My early years saw me growing up and taking my first steps in the capital city, Harare. This is also where, three years after I arrived, my sister, Leigh, was born.

Shortly after the war, my dad took the deputy head teacher's post at a primary school situated in the north-east of the city.

I grew up in peace time. Rationing was still biting hard and things were in short supply, but I didn't know any different. People were friendly and life was good. Times were changing, and the country's prosperity was increasing.

I attended an infants' school that was just a walk over the playing field away from home, as we lived on the school grounds. I remember my teacher used to knock on the chalkboard with the wooden handle of the board rubber and 'magically' there would be a knock in return.

She told us it was the fairies who were knocking, and my six-year-old mind believed her.

Because we lived on site, I would run around the school grounds freely out of hours, happily occupying myself with building dams in the puddles, climbing trees and having conversations with the man who drove the school tractor. I would help our gardener harvest avocado pears the size of pineapples from the massive tree in our garden. He used a long bamboo pole with a bent coat hanger at one end that resembled a hook and another coat hanger attached underneath the hook that was in a hoop shape. The hoop had an old fertiliser bag attached to it so that as an avocado's stem was tugged by the hook it would fall into the bag and be saved from smashing into a million pieces on the ground below.

It was from one of these tall trees in the garden that a vital piece of African playground equipment was hung. A couple of ropes secured to a branch held an old car tyre that had been turned inside out and fashioned into a seat with two arching handles where the rope attached. A swing.

Occasionally I had the opportunity to indulge in a treat. Counting up my coins, I would walk to the school gate with my mother, as a particular ice-cream man knew this was a good spot to sell his wares. Wearing their dark-blue uniforms, which consisted of a floppy hat, a long-sleeved button-up shirt and grey trousers with a blue stripe down the side, the army of ice-cream men and women would cycle around the city on their specially adapted three-wheeled bicycles. Attached above the two smaller front wheels was an insulated box filled with ice creams and dry ice. This meant that when the box was opened it was always accompanied by a puff of dry ice smoke, which added to the drama and pleasure of the event. This particular ice-cream man was on to a good thing as he sold quite a few ice creams at the school gates over the years.

I loved the joy an ice-cream man brought to people. So much, in fact, that all through my primary school years it was my life's ambition to become one myself one day.

In 1987, my dad was offered a once-in-a-lifetime opportunity to become a headmaster and to open a brand-new school about an hour's drive to the north of Harare.

On our first visit to the location of where the new school would be built, my mother packed a feast for the epic journey: sandwiches, cola in glass bottles, boiled sweets and a wet flannel tucked away in a plastic bag. We all climbed into the family car, a dark blue Renault 4, which had a gear stick in the shape of an upturned L coming out of the dashboard, and not much suspension. So we jiggled about as we drove along.

It was exciting, going to visit the place that would become our new home, not knowing what to expect.

After driving for what seemed like forever, we finally stopped opposite a small, rundown building on the side of the road. It was a simple structure made of brick, with a tin roof. It stocked some household essentials as well as alcohol. Out in the countryside of Zimbabwe, these stores were the corner shop and the local bar rolled into one. It was also not uncommon to see chickens scratching in the dust outside these establishments, as well as some people waiting for the bus who had been there for a day or two.

We got out of the car and stepped over a thin length of a barbed wire fence that was about knee-high. The elephant grass towered above my head, and my sister's, as we carved our way through the virgin African bush. There was also an abundance of msasa trees in this area, whose leaves turn a variety of rusty reds and yellows in autumn.

After walking for a while, not really being able to see much as the grass was so tall, we stopped and Dad said, 'Here is where the office is going to be,' and, 'Here is where the dormitories will go.' After venturing deeper into the grass, he stopped and proudly announced, 'This is where our new house will be built.'

It was hard to imagine that a school would rise out of the ground on this spot; the tall grass giving way to manicured lawns, office blocks, classrooms, playgrounds, a swimming pool, tennis courts, playing fields and dormitories. But it did.

In 1988, the school opened its doors and my sister and I were two of the original eighty-six founding members of Barwick School.

As well as receiving a great education, I had many adventures there.

One of these was an early flurry into the world of the entrepreneur. In my upper primary school years, I set up a small business raising and selling chickens. It operated out of our utility room and the chicken coop was erected next to the carport. I would buy fifty chicks that were a day old, and then raise them into fully fledged adult birds. The gardener helped and was paid in kind; he would get a couple of chickens at the end of that brood. It was good fun and I learned quite a few things about running a business along the way.

Being located out in the 'bush', as Zimbabweans would call it, the wilds of Africa were quite literally on our doorstep. I'm not talking about lions sleeping on the patio or elephants roaming through the garden. You would need to go to a safari park to encounter animals like that. But you did get some amazing wildlife.

Around Christmas-time in particular, a type of beetle would emerge in its thousands – hence the name 'Christmas beetles'. Most were about the same size and shape of a peanut but you would occasionally find some giant-sized ones about the size of a domino piece. They would all swarm around the lights at night and quite a few would die, so you would need to sweep them up in the morning.

There were also several close encounters with deadly snakes, like the time when a black mamba had hidden itself underneath the piano in our hallway and my dad had to dispatch it with a golf club. Or the time when the security guards came running to our house to fetch help because they had encountered a six-metre-long green mamba in one of the trees of the school. Eventually it was scared off and it slithered away into the bush without harming anyone. Then there was the time when a farmer and some of his workforce arrived in a lorry. It pulled up on the school field and dumped a massive python onto the grass. It had just eaten a large antelope – you could see its hooves and legs pressing through from inside the enormous snake's body – so the farmer thought the children might want to have a look. We did!

My interest in music and singing was also taking hold. I have loved listening to music and singing for as long as I can remember. At primary school I was part of the school choir. One highlight was when the choir all climbed into the school bus and went to Harare, in 1991, to a recording studio for a day. Our choir mistress was recording a song and wanted the school choir to sing on the recording. It was an amazing experience. I still recall her telling us that the day was going to be very special, and that we should do our best to enjoy the experience because not many of us would get the opportunity to sing in a recording studio again. The studio housed a couple of soundproofed rooms, a mixing desk and a reel-to-reel recorder. I thoroughly enjoyed the process and hoped that it would not be the last time I set foot in a recording studio.

I was having piano lessons. I did not enjoy them very much and I hardly ever did any practising. As a result, progress was tough and extremely limited, which in turn did not really inspire me to enjoy the process more. However, at that age I was in no position to complain. Or perhaps I did complain but I didn't manage to get out of it.

It was near the end of my primary education that my mother had a chat with the piano teacher and arranged for me to have a go at learning to play the guitar instead. I had been given a nylon-stringed guitar as a present, so I had something to play on. Having no previous experience of playing a guitar, I had my first lesson. It was hard. I just couldn't get the idea of how to strum, and my fingers were no good at making the chord shapes and most certainly weren't able to press the strings down hard enough. It was a disaster. I remember hating it and I knew that the teacher felt just as frustrated. She told my mother that I would never be able to play the guitar – which is ironic as now I play the guitar as part of my career. In a rage, the guitar got thrown to the back of my wardrobe, never to see the light of day for many years.

One of my annual highlights growing up was going on one of my father's Adventure Tours.[2] Children who were just about to enter their final year of primary school spent a weekend at Adventure Tour, based at the school. However, it was a weekend unlike any other. Everyone was split into teams that were called 'patrols' and competed by doing various challenges.

My dad had spent the previous months preparing, and there was an impressive ropes course constructed within the trees – suspended car tyres that moved as you clambered through, rope bridges and other obstacles that concluded with a rapid descent down a zip line. Each patrol had a T-shirt that showed off their team's colour. They also had fun screen-printing the Adventure Tour logo and their patrol name onto it in an art lesson in the weeks leading up to the event.

Each patrol was given a set ration of food. It was up to them how they distributed, cooked and used the food over the weekend. We cooked in our patrols over open fires that we had to collect wood for, build and light. We also had to do our own washing up. We slept in sleeping bags under the stars, or in the school hall if it was raining.

---

[2] An activity weekend my father organised. It was not a registered organisation and the logo was designed by my father on a piece of cardboard that he cut into a stencil – just a bit of fun, really.

Other activities included things like how fast the patrol could change the tyre of a car, or the whole team had to climb a tree and then proceed to build and light a fire in the tree in order to boil some water and make the supervising teacher a cup of tea. Another activity was using various tyre tubes, ropes and planks of wood to construct a raft in order to transport one member of the team who had been designated the 'injured' person. The objective was to get them safely across the length of the pool without getting them wet.

All this was great fun and taught us a lot about teamwork, communication, risk and adventure.

Attending the same school where your father is the headmaster and your mother is a teacher has its challenges. I really wanted to get things right and to be 'good'. I understood that I had to set an example, as other children would be looking at me as the son of the headmaster to see how I did things. It was for this reason that I tried my best to always do the right thing, to always 'colour within the lines'.

Despite this pressure, life was good. The school hall was impressive and had a steeply sloping roof to one side. It overlooked the Great Dyke mountain range on the other side of the valley, and I would often catch myself looking at this view and thinking how lucky I was to be growing up in a place like that.

By this time, the country had entered a golden age. Crops were flourishing and were being exported all over the world. There was plenty of food on the shelves of the supermarkets too; people would get excited about discovering new and exotic things that were imported from foreign countries, which were starting to appear in the more affluent areas of the cities. Tourists were visiting in droves and the country's infrastructure was working well. There was running water in the taps, rubbish was collected weekly, hospitals had medicines and there was electricity.

Now, this is not to say that the problem of poverty was solved. It most certainly was not. There were still people who were poor, people who begged on the streets and would offer to look after your car in the supermarket car park in exchange for a 'tip' of a few coins when you returned.

In parts of the countryside, massive farms employed workforces of hundreds, who were given healthcare, housing and education for their children. But there were other areas where the land was not as productive and the rains not as plentiful. Here you would find mud and pole huts with their characteristic cylindrical exteriors and straw roofs that looked like traditional conical Chinese hats perched on top of them.

Life was hard here, yet you would be greeted with massive smiles. Hope was not lost.

2
Peterhouse Powerhouse

The state-run education system in Zimbabwe was not good. It was generally accepted that if you wanted an education that was of any value, you would have to attend an independent (private) school, and these cost money. I was fortunate that my father was a headmaster as this meant that paying for my secondary education was taken care of, as it was paid for by his school (it was part of the perks he received). I was able to choose my own secondary school and I went along to several open days at possible schools that were within about two to three hours' drive from home. I could have gone to a school further away, but this would have made transportation difficult and further limited my ability to see my family.

All private secondary schools in Zimbabwe were boarding schools. I did not have a choice about boarding – it's just what you did.

After looking at several options, I decided Peterhouse was my school of choice. Now all I had to do was pass the selective entrance examination.

It was a nervous endeavour. Having never particularly got on with numbers, I was particularly concerned about the mathematics paper.

I remember walking into the large and imposing hall and sitting at my designated table. This was actually a purpose-built theatre, but today it was an examination hall, and the highly polished stage displayed a clock and a desk for the invigilators to use.

The exam consisted of a few different papers that all went by in a flash and a blur. A few months later the results were announced, and I was informed that I had indeed been offered a place. I was overjoyed.

Next came the wait to see which boarding house I would be assigned to. These were where you would stay, with dormitories, ablution blocks, etc, but also were the team you would be in for sports, academic and other competitions. Your house was an important part of your school identity. So much so that when we wore our khaki uniform that consisted of a brown, short-sleeved, button-up shirt with collar, brown shorts cut above the knee and long, knee-length brown socks, the elastic garters we wore to hold up our socks had to have a ribbon that was in our house colour that would stick out below the overturned sock on the side of the calf.

All I wanted to do was to fit in. To be accepted. To survive.

I remember the first day of boarding school in 1992. As I was being dropped off I saw a fully grown man emerge from another car dressed in school uniform – at least that is what he looked like to my young eyes. I couldn't quite believe that I was going to have to rub shoulders with others at the school who were so huge.

I took a deep breath and found my dormitory and got settled in.

Over the coming weeks, I was on an extremely steep learning curve. I learned how to navigate life in a completely unfamiliar system where there was a set of written school rules as well as an unwritten code of language and a hierarchy established and enforced by the student body themselves.

I quickly understood that if I used bad language, this was one way I could blend in, as everyone else was swearing constantly. So I started following the crowd simply to fit in and be accepted while feeling quite uncomfortable doing so – it wasn't who I was.

The school was Anglican. There was a resident chaplain who led the services in the warehouse-sized chapel built with large granite stones, cemented together to form an impressively imposing structure. The services were compulsory, so we attended every Sunday and again during the week on our age group's designated day. It was a formal and traditional affair complete with candles, liturgy, ancient hymns and flowing robes.

Within the first couple of weeks, there were try-outs for the choir. I desperately wanted to be in the choir as I knew that I enjoyed singing, and having a front row seat also had its appeal. I did my best and within a few days I learned that I had indeed been accepted into the choir. I needed to attend rehearsals three times a week and have a fitting for a choir robe.

I remained a faithful choir member throughout my senior school career. It was here I found that the words to many of the ancient hymns jumped out at me and caused me to think.

Like all boarding schools, the daily routine and timetable established the rhythm of life. These were often inflexible, and obviously some parts of the schedule were a lot less enjoyable than others. Homework sessions were one of these not-so-enjoyable times. Every evening for two hours we would sit in silence at our hard, wooden desks to do homework, or read a book, or stare at the walls. We had the chance for a quick ten-minute break after the first hour, then it was back to homework again until the bell rang. There was no use trying to fight the system, as a big and burly sixth-form prefect supervised each room and ensured strict adherence to the rules.

Only a few months after starting senior school, George Nheweyembwa, the guy who slept in the bed next to mine in the dormitory, gave me an opportunity I couldn't miss. He asked if I wanted to skip the evening homework session on Thursday. I could hardly believe that such a thing was possible. It sounded like heaven. To make it even more inviting, he also told me that there was a cup of coffee in it for me afterwards.

Let's just say it didn't take much convincing for me to agree to go along to whatever it was George had invited me to. I hadn't thought much about what we would actually be doing instead of homework; just escaping the confines of the silence and boredom was enough for me.

As homework began, George and I set off in the darkness of early evening. We strolled across the campus with the complete knowledge and permission of the powers-that-be, who were made aware of our whereabouts that evening in advance. We arrived at the foyer of the hall we were heading for, and to my surprise it was packed full of about 200 other homework escapees from all over the school. Different ages, different houses, yet all wearing the same regulation navy blue school tracksuit.

The atmosphere was friendly and expectant, a camaraderie of the sort I had not experienced before. I soon got the idea that this was a Christian group, but I had no idea what I was in for. After a short prayer, the singing began. This was the strangest thing I had experienced in my young life. For a start, the enthusiastic young teacher at the front who was leading the meeting took out a guitar and began to play and sing. I had no idea that you could sing along to a guitar at a Christian meeting. Surely there were rules about that sort of thing? The other boys joined in with gusto and loud, raucous singing filled the air. They were clapping along and lifting up their hands – it was weird, and it slightly unnerved me. I wasn't sure that this sort of thing was for me at all. I politely tried to sing along, but I was determined to keep my hands firmly where they were, folded in front of me.

Then the teacher talked about a passage in the Bible and we prayed. That bit was a little more bearable, but I was still very glad to get out into the fresh night air after it was all over. At that point, I certainly did not think I would be going back again.

However, George was persistent, and he continued to ask if I would like to join him on a Thursday evening. I liked George and I hated homework, so the following Thursday I found myself back in the hall's foyer. This time I knew what to expect, and the singing, clapping and guitar playing didn't seem as strange as it had the first time.

The Thursday evening meeting soon became a regular fixture for me. After a while, I felt comfortable enough to join in with the clapping, and my singing became more exuberant. I was also learning a lot from the Bible talks and again I found myself thinking more deeply about God, just like when I sang the hymns in chapel. I had a lot of questions and I was starting to find the answers to some of them.

It was a crisp, clear Zimbabwean winter's evening in July 1992. We had arrived back at school for the second term and the rugby season was in full swing. The faint smell of woodsmoke hung in the chilly air. As the sun went down, the cold could really bite, and in buildings equipped for the heat of summer rather than the chill of winter, with stone floors and single-glazed windows, we needed to bundle up to keep warm. A tracksuit, thick jumper, woolly hat and scarf would suffice.

But tonight something different was going on. All day there had been a bustle of activity. Tractors and trailers were seen moving the supporter stands from alongside the first team rugby touchline and relocating them to the vast open space situated in front of the school chapel that was usually quite tranquil and covered in paved walkways and neatly manicured lawns. On the raised walkway just beneath the main entrance there were lighting rigs, a drum kit, keyboards and metre upon metre of cables.

As night fell, I discovered that we had another compulsory event to attend, but this time I really wanted to go. A rock band formed by one of the school's old boys while he was at university in Cape Town had returned to the school to give a concert.

The atmosphere was electric. The senior boys occupied the stands to the back of the audience area. I was in the crowd that massed along the base of the stairs that led up to the raised walkway where the band was situated. The staff common room was in a large building to the side, and staff members could be seen climbing out of the common room windows to sit on the flat roof in order to watch. Some even managed to squeeze a few chairs out of the windows.

Then the concert began. The music blasted out and the spotlights swung skyward and picked out the lead singer, who was standing on a ledge right near the roof of the chapel, which was about 10m high, as he belted out the first song.

The fun continued with lots of humorous songs as well as a few serious ones mixed in. Near the end of the concert, the band took a break and the lead singer spent about ten minutes explaining that we were all sinners, we had all got it wrong and had done things that were not pleasing to God and that the penalty we should pay for this was death and eternal separation from God. He explained that God loved us so much that He sent Jesus, His Son, to pay that penalty for us. Jesus died in our place, to take our sins from us to enable us to get right with God and to live a life with Him and for Him.

The lead singer then asked us to bow our heads and to put up our hand if we wanted to give our lives to Jesus. Right there and then, without hesitation and with tears streaming down my face, I knew what I had to do. I really wanted to do it. All my questioning and searching for answers had led me to this point, to this moment. I put up my hand and prayed the prayer along with the lead singer as he prayed one sentence at a time. I gave my life to Jesus that night, standing there in the cold night air surrounded by hundreds of my peers who were at a rock concert. My entire life changed in that moment.

I knew what I had done. I had raised my hand in a crowd and prayed a prayer but I didn't dare tell anyone else about the decision I had made. After all, I still had that deep need for survival and acceptance.

I continued to go along to the Christian group on a Thursday evening, as well as serve as part of the choir in the more traditional setting.

About two weeks after the rock concert, I was in the dormitory when something happened that caused me to swear. I can't remember exactly what it was, but I do remember the reaction of one of the other boys whom I didn't get along with particularly well. With a rather shocked look on his face he said, 'You can't say that. You're a Christian!' This really caught me off guard. I hadn't told anyone about my decision, yet this guy who didn't even know me very well thought it was quite obvious. How did he know? Maybe the change within me was working itself out in how I behaved. After that point,

I wasn't afraid to tell people that I was a Christian because they all seemed to know anyway.

One of the big driving forces of the school was sporting prowess. A big deal was made of those who represented the school in the first team of whatever sport was played, but in particular the first fifteen rugby team were prized above all others. They were treated a bit like celebrities and, indeed, some went on to play international rugby for various countries around the world. Various students have also gone on to participate at the Olympics for other sporting disciplines.

It was quite common for positions of responsibility within the school, such as prefects and heads of houses, to be given to those who excelled at sport. In fact, it was almost unheard of for it to be otherwise.

The school also placed a high regard upon academic achievement.

This presented me with a couple of problems. First, I was absolutely rubbish at playing sport, and to be honest, sport still has a negative effect on me when I think about it now. Contact sports scare me. Yet here I was within a culture that celebrated and rewarded sporting ability and achievement.

Second, I was not one of the brightest academic minds to have walked the face of the planet. I really struggled with mathematics and was very glad to achieve a pass at O level[3] as this meant I could drop the subject. In English, my spelling was terrible. I even had a French teacher threaten to stop teaching the subject if I continued with it.

---

[3] O levels or GCEs were the examinations before GCSEs.

Needless to say, I was more than happy to drop French too.

The pathway to success and achievement at school, therefore, seemed to be set and clear. However, I took a different route. Nothing motivated me more than the things I enjoyed doing: singing, music, acting – and caring for others. I soon found ways of doing the things I loved, as there were opportunities for these too.

One of the things I loathed was 'supporting' the first team, which involved hours of standing in the cold along the sidelines of a muddy rugby pitch singing endless chants and war cries, quite often with a big senior stood in front, blocking my view of the whole game. So I trained in first aid and became a first aider. I was now positioned on the opposite side of the field, with a great front-row seat. I also got to go onto the pitch and patch people up. Sometimes, if it was really bad, I would even have to have strong words with the teacher who was the coach, who obviously needed his valuable player back in the game, yet I needed to get him to a hospital. I became a valued member of the rugby team and sometimes travelled with them to away fixtures.

Over the years, I became more involved in the pastoral and spiritual side of school life. I became one of the main leaders of the Thursday Christian group and even taught myself how to play guitar to help it continue when the teacher who led it went to work at a different school. After a time, I also become one of the leaders who helped to make plans and decisions for the group as well as give talks about the Bible.

At the end of my fifth year, I was recognised by the school by being awarded the highest honour the school could give – an 'Honours Tie', which was a silver tie with small blue crowns embroidered on it. Not many people were awarded one of those, let alone in the fifth form.

In my final year, to much astonishment, I was appointed as head of my house, and held a variety of other leadership positions within the school. Owing to the fact that I was in charge of so much, I quickly found the necessity and art of delegation, stepping in where I needed to, but enabling others to function and do the work in my stead.

For the final couple of years, the question that was nagging everyone at that stage was, 'What do I want to do for the rest of my life?' This inevitably led me to thinking about whether higher education was in fact an option for me or not.

I was not very clear on what I wanted to do as a career. As well as doing something that I enjoyed, there were other important things to consider.

For the past decade or so, Zimbabwe had enjoyed economic prosperity. Food and supplies were in abundance in the shops. Tourism was booming and agricultural exports were doing really well, all leading to a flow of foreign currency in and out of the economy. Things were stable and life was good. However, as I entered my final year at senior school, things were starting to take a turn for the worse.

The president of Zimbabwe, Robert Mugabe, had promised those who had fought alongside him in the liberation war land in exchange for their loyalty and sacrifice. It had been many years since the civil war and independence when he had made these promises, and now his supporters were getting restless. They had not received the land they had been promised. There was unease and his power was being threatened. In response, Mugabe sanctioned the forcible removal of white farmers (as those with white skin were the enemy in the war days) from their hugely profitable multi-million-dollar-generating farms. These were then parcelled up and randomly divided between those who invaded it.

Not only were the white farmers removed, or sometimes murdered, but the entire workforce of several hundred per farm were also displaced. The new inhabitants of the land were subsistence farmers, only growing enough for themselves and their families. The machinery needed to produce crops on an industrial scale was mostly destroyed or sold. So the rapid decline of the Zimbabwean economy began. In one swift move the two biggest income generators for the nation, namely agricultural exports and tourism, were killed off.

The land invasions, as they became known, had just started when I was entering my final year of school – there was a lot worse to come. But even by this stage it was clear that the future in Zimbabwe was not as certain as it once had been. Before now, I had never had any intention of living anywhere else, but now I was faced with life-altering decisions.

By now, I had three loves: my first-aid activities, an ability to teach, and God. Taking these into account, I chose my very unusual combination of A level subjects: biology (in case I wanted to be a paramedic), literature (in case I wanted to become a teacher) and divinity[4] (in case I wanted to work for the Church).

As things in the country were changing, I thought it would be wise to get a university degree to help my employment prospects in general, but also if I needed to leave the country to find work elsewhere. This led to another conundrum. Money. Or should I say, lack of it. I was extremely fortunate that my parents were both teachers, as my education was paid for by the school they worked for. However, this was not the case for university education. An added complication was that Zimbabwe did not really have any decent higher education institutions – at least, not ones that provided a qualification that was recognised and carried some weight outside the country. I would have to go and study abroad if I wanted a university degree. Obviously, this added to the cost.

There were no such things as student loans in Zimbabwe, so I applied for a bursary. At the time there was a group of independent schools called the Association of Trust Schools (ATS) who offered a bursary to train teachers who would then in turn work for a member school for a set period of time. If you had four years of university, you were bonded to work for a member school of its choice for the same amount of time in exchange. Things in the country had only just started on their downward trajectory, and at this time I was quite optimistic that things would be alright in the long term. So I could go to university and have a degree and a career at

---

[4] Another name for Religious Studies, but a field that only focuses on Christianity.

the end of it. Both my parents were primary school teachers so I knew exactly what I was getting myself into. It was not my first choice of career but I knew it was a job that I could do, and I also figured that it was one that could be transferable to pretty much any country in the world.

I was thrilled when I was invited to the next step of the interview process a couple of months later. As it turned out, I was one of four chosen to be awarded with an ATS bursary to attend Rhodes University in the neighbouring country of South Africa. ATS even agreed to defer my entry to university as I was hoping to go to the UK on a gap year.

Leaving Peterhouse was a time of mixed emotions. I had not only survived but thrived there. I had done a lot of growing up and had become my own person. I was a respected member of society who many looked up to. In some ways I was sad to go, yet at the same time I was desperate to leave, to spread my wings and take flight into the big wide world. Adventure awaited and I was ready to jump headlong into it.

I spent the next year in the UK working as a teaching assistant, a wine bar tender and a kitchen porter (washing the dishes!) in a restaurant. I also did a bit of busking on the streets with my guitar. I travelled around the country taking in the sights and even spent two weeks on the west coast of France in the summer.

During that year I found it very difficult to find a church that was 'alive'. Maybe it was the area in which I was located, but I found it hard. As a result, the year saw me begin to drift away from God in heart and in action.

3
City of Saints

It was January 1999, the height of summer in the southern hemisphere. I had made my way across the sun-baked tarmac of Harare International Airport and had climbed the portable staircase up into the plane. Out of my window I could see a heat haze in the distance along the runway where a couple of cattle egrets were fluttering and strutting about in search of insects.

Once the plane had eventually filled up with the rest of its passengers, we took off, heading towards Cape Town, South Africa, a journey of 1,550 miles[5] which would take us about three and a half hours.

It was quite common to strike up polite conversation with strangers in Zimbabwe, so it did not surprise me when the gentleman next to me introduced himself and we started chatting. He told me that he was involved in some sort of church work, but the conversation centred more on me and where I was going. I explained that I had spent the past year in the UK on a gap year and now I was heading off to university for the first time. We spoke a bit

---

[5] Around 2,500km.

about Christianity, and I mentioned that I had found the past year very difficult in this regard. For some reason I found it quite easy to talk to this man about these things in a comfortable and natural way. It wasn't awkward at all. Perhaps it was that he was a stranger, or maybe there was more of a divine hand in our chance encounter than I could imagine.

Near the end of our flight, he asked if he could pray for me. I agreed. He asked God to help me at university and to quickly lead me to a church and group of friends who loved Jesus and who would encourage me and help me in my faith.

This was a special and significant encounter for me. It showed me that despite my wanderings, God was still with me and wanted to draw me back to Himself. It warmed my heart and helped to calm some of my nervousness about this new chapter of life that I was about to begin.

My grandparents were at the airport to meet me, and they helped me to pack my belongings into the car. They had lived in Cape Town for many years, and I was quite familiar with the city and surrounding towns owing to many holidays spent visiting them.

A few days later we set off along the east coast, along South Africa's 'Garden Route' as they drove me up to Rhodes University in the city of Grahamstown.[6]

I had arrived a week before lectures were due to begin for Orientation Week ('O' Week), a time for newcomers to settle in, become familiar with their surroundings, register with the university and start to make new friends.

---

[6] In 2018 the city's name was officially changed to Makhanda.

I soon learned that a nickname for Grahamstown was the 'City of Saints' owing to its many churches located within a relatively small area. However, life on the university campus looked more like a city of sinners at first glance.

One of the first things I was handed when I set foot on campus and was shown to my room in the boarding house was an orientation pack. From my conservative Zimbabwean upbringing I was very surprised to find that in among the leaflets, maps and booklets there was also a supply of condoms included.

Thankfully, it was not long before the man on the plane's prayer was answered. A day or two after my arrival I was wandering around campus, trying to find the location of a certain lecture hall to hear the dean introduce their subject and faculty. I suddenly saw a face I recognised. It was Paul Nyamuda.

Paul was a great friend from boarding school. He was a strong Christian, and someone I had looked up to. He was a couple of years my senior, but this hadn't stopped a friendship from forming. I was so pleased to see him. It turned out that he was going to a great, lively church in Grahamstown – one that a couple of hundred students attended. After a good catch-up conversation, we exchanged contact details as well as the time and place where the church was meeting that Sunday. I was determined to go along to check it out. In fact, I had already decided that based on what I knew of Paul, I didn't have to look for another church in the city. If he was going to this church, that was a good enough endorsement for me.

At last Sunday came, and the church was all I hoped it would be. It was called His People Christian Church[7] and was part of an international university campus ministry that had started in Cape Town. The singing was lively, the Bible teaching was relevant and engaging and I could clearly feel the Holy Spirit being present. I very quickly got involved in a variety of ways.

There was so much that the church had to offer, and I wanted to do everything, from Bible School on Tuesday evenings to small groups on Wednesday and band rehearsal on Thursday. I was growing spiritually, and I loved it – I just wanted more and more.

I made a lot of friends, most from within the church, and we spent a lot of time together.

You would think that a heavy church schedule would mean my university work would suffer, but somehow it didn't. I found I could do both, and ended up doing well with my studies.

I only had three years at Rhodes and the time flew by. As I was nearing my final year, leadership positions opened up quite naturally for me again. I was appointed as the church's ambassador and liaison with the university and was appointed chairperson of the His People Society on campus. I was also one of the band leaders at the church and had my own group of musicians and singers to lead and pastor. However, I knew time was short, and pretty much as soon as I was appointed, I was already training up my successor.

---

[7] Since my time at university, His People has changed its name to Every Nation, Grahamstown.

I had also begun to dabble in the world of songwriting and had penned a few worship songs that the church pastor and other musicians were very encouraging about. Looking back now, those songs weren't that great, but I am extremely grateful for the encouragement and belief in my talents as a songwriter, as this caused me to want to grow and improve in this area. I even got some of the band together and we recorded my first single, 'Jewel of Africa', in a home studio in Grahamstown (which was actually someone's living room that smelled of old cigarettes).

Around this time, I was starting to seriously look for a wife. I had had a few relationships in my teenage years; however, none of them were particularly serious. I believe the longest amount of time any of those relationships had lasted was roughly two weeks. There were many other girls who had caught my eye but invariably they did not return my affections. Over time this wore me down and really hurt, so much so that I started to believe that I was unlovable and that it would be impossible for me to ever get married and have a family of my own.

I wanted to marry the girl that God had in mind for me. I wanted to do things His way and to live my life where He was in charge and not me. I was learning that doing things God's way was much better than trying to do whatever I thought was best. The decision of who to marry was a very serious and important one, and I didn't want to get it wrong.

There was one girl in particular who was a year lower than me at university who I took a shine to. I spent a lot of time with her and she came to my church. I prayed long and hard as to whether she was indeed the girl for me. In the end I received a strong word from God, which was simply, 'Wait'. This calmed my searching and seeking for a while as I was content that God was on the case, that He did indeed have someone special for me but it wasn't the right time. I just had to be obedient – and wait.

4
Zimbabwe

My final postgraduate year of university was not spent at Rhodes in South Africa. Because the economic situation in Zimbabwe was worsening by the day, those in charge of the teaching bursary scheme made the decision that all those in their fourth year would complete their final year in the capital of Zimbabwe, Harare, as this made more economic sense for them.

This meant that accommodation could be sourced cheaply as students could be posted at member schools for little to no cost, and we were enrolled to complete our postgraduate certificates of education (PGCE) via correspondence with the University of South Africa (UNISA), which is a distance-learning institution, very similar to the Open University in the UK. As a bonus, we had extra classes and lectures at a local teacher training college based in Harare, which also acted as our contact with the UNISA syllabus.

I was posted to a primary school and spent many days gaining teacher training experience both in the classroom and on the sports field. I had a little room above one of the classrooms and I could walk across the playing fields to the senior school boarding houses for my meals.

Harare was a big place. This posed a problem as I did not have any form of transport, nor did I have lots of money to spend on taxis. As a result, I bought a bicycle.

The bicycle helped to widen my reach within the city and I was able to get to most places where I needed to be, even if it meant missing breakfast in the morning to complete the sixty-minute cycle to get to my lectures on time.

I had many adventures on that bicycle. As I was hand-washing all my clothes in the bath, I needed somewhere to dry them. Several blocks away, one of the street vendors was selling woodwork items on the side of the road. One of the things he sold was a wooden, collapsible clothes horse – this was just what I was looking for. One weekend, I cycled over and bought the clothes horse, which I balanced precariously and rather uncomfortably over one shoulder while I cycled back to where I was living, wobbling all the way. I had to keep stopping to swap shoulders as they started to ache after a while.

On another occasion, I was at a shopping centre and the pocket of my shorts caught on a door handle as I walked past, almost completely ripping my shorts off. That day I had to fight back the embarrassment as I cycled home along the main road, shorts flapping in the breeze, just barely keeping my dignity intact.

Upon my arrival in Harare, I made it my business to quickly find and get involved in a church. Now, there are many to choose from in Harare, so where to begin? Well, my friend Paul had moved back to Harare a year or so before me, so – you guessed it – I went to the church where he was involved. It was called Hear the Word.[8] This was to be my first experience of being part of a mega-church.

The church had heard from Paul that I was a musician and singer, and so I found my fit quickly. I was part of a small group with some of the musicians from the church and was attending band rehearsals within the first couple of weeks of my arrival. Shortly afterwards I was on the rota of the worship band, playing acoustic guitar in front of a congregation of thousands for three back-to-back services on most Sundays. Of course, this meant quite a lot of travelling. You would often find me on my bicycle going from one place to the other with a rucksack on my back that held my guitar case, sticking out of the top.

During this time, my musicianship grew a lot. I had some guitar lessons to help me improve my playing. I also had the privilege of being able to run some of my compositions past some serious musicians and songwriters whose songs were topping the charts at the time. During that year, I teamed up with a friend and re-released the single 'Jewel of Africa' that I had recorded in South Africa the year before, and it got some radio airplay as well as a spot on the Zimbabwean charts.

During my year in Harare, the political and economic instability within the country continued to increase at a rapid rate. The state-sponsored Land Reform Programme had encouraged bloody scenes outside many farmhouses with baying mobs chanting and attacking the inhabitants – forcing them off the land and out of their homes. Some were murdered, many severely injured. Farms were set

---

[8] It has since changed its name to Celebration Church International.

ablaze, and livestock slaughtered. This happened under the gaze of the police force who stood by and watched, only arresting those who tried to stop the madness. White people were branded as enemies of the state by the president. The atmosphere in the country was very tense and uncomfortable, and this only grew as things deteriorated even further over the years that followed.

These events triggered a massive economic collapse, which saw the value of the Zimbabwean dollar destroyed by rampant inflation. In fact, Zimbabwe holds the record for the second largest[9] hyper-inflation rate the world has ever seen, which reached 79.6 billion per cent at its height. This saw prices doubling every twenty-four hours.[10]

At the end of 2002, my time in Harare finished, as I had completed my studies and I was now being posted to one of the member-schools to begin my four years of paying back my debt to the bursary scheme.

I was posted to Bulawayo, the second largest city in Zimbabwe, but a six-hour drive away. I needed a car. Having passed my driving test some years previously, I was able to drive, but owning a car was a luxury not many could afford. At this time I was fortunate enough to be able to use some of the foreign currency I had in a bank account in the UK to buy one. However, acquiring petrol to run the car was exceptionally challenging, as absolutely everything – from petrol to toilet rolls – was in short supply. Even cash itself was being rationed by the banks.

---

[9] The highest inflation rate was seen in Hungary in 1946.
[10] https://www.cnbc.com/2011/02/14/The-Worst-Hyperinflation-Situations-of-All-Time.html (accessed 14th June 2021).

Unfortunately, I did not enjoy the school I was assigned to. As soon as I had begun, I was making plans as to how I could 'escape'. It was so depressing and I was desperately unhappy.

I had nowhere to live. I did not know anyone in the city. The country was in meltdown. However, a different school, located on the other side of the city, came to my rescue. It provided me with full board and lodging in exchange for me coaching one afternoon of sport per week. This was a blessing. Looking back on it, I can really see that God was at work in this amazing act of generosity and kindness. At the time, however, I was still trying to keep my head above water and did not really notice the enormity of it.

Most weekends were spent queuing outside the bank to withdraw my allocated amount of rationed cash. There was a shortage of cash owing to the escalating prices, so we were only allowed a certain amount per week. There was no such thing as 'plastic' – no credit or debit cards. Because the economy was in meltdown, no one accepted cheques. So we would leave the bank with our 'bricks' of cash – wads of Z$500 notes tied together with elastic bands so that they looked a bit like bricks.

My first pay cheque was more than 1 million Zimbabwean dollars; however, I was still living below the poverty line. This was not even enough to buy groceries – and I was employed!

Once I had finally got hold of some cash, it was another queuing exercise at the supermarket. Hours later, one might walk away with a few bread rolls, as flour was in short supply. The supermarket shelves were bare. You would buy the little of what was available, if you could. There was no change in the tills, which meant I would be offered a couple of peppermints or some fruit that was past its sell-by date as change instead.

Another weekend pastime was sitting in the car. Not on a nice weekend drive, but parked up along the side of the road in a queue of cars and trucks waiting for an elusive delivery of fuel to one or other petrol station, which may or may not arrive. We took our chances and waited. My record was staying in a petrol queue for four days. Others endured a lot longer. It came to a point where the fuel situation was so bad that I parked the car where I was staying and resorted to waking up at 4am to cycle to get to work on time at the other side of the city.

Something had to give. I was miserable. I had come to realise that there was no future for me in Zimbabwe. How could I provide for a family in these conditions? It was a daily struggle to keep myself alive, let alone to be responsible for anyone else.

The situation in the country continued to worsen. Then family friends got in touch and said that they had some foreign currency outside the country that they wanted to lend me, interest free, to buy myself out of the bursary deal with the school. I jumped at the chance.

My grandfather came from the UK, so I could apply for an Ancestry Visa to go to live and work there. Endless forms were filled in. The passport and the payment of millions of Zimbabwean dollars were sent to the British High Commission. Now all I could do was wait.

After a few weeks I received bad news. The British High Commission had rejected my application. This was a blow. Then it occurred to me that I had been so busy pursuing my own agenda, I had not stopped to ask God if this was what He wanted for my life. This realisation punched me in the gut.

I fell to my knees and apologised to God. I learned that once I had decided to follow Jesus, I was His; He was now in control. He was the one in the driving seat, not me – I go where He wants me to go and do what He wants me to do, not what I feel like doing. I told Him that I would go where He wanted me to go and if that was not to be the UK, then that was fine. I would trust Him with my life and my future, no matter where it led.

Then a miracle happened.

The very next day I received a phone call from the British High Commission. They told me that they had changed their mind, as a relative in the UK had sent them a document they needed, and that my application was now approved. All I had to do was post my passport back to them at no extra cost and they would give me the visa.

This was unheard of. The British High Commission never changed their mind! Once you were rejected, that was it. There was no going back and there were no second chances. But when God is in control – anything is possible.

5
Starting Again

A couple of months later, I stepped off the plane at London's Heathrow Airport with that same rucksack I had been cycling around Harare with on my back, a guitar in my hand and £12 in my pocket.

It felt amazing.

The most noticeable thing I felt was a complete sense of freedom. I was not afraid of making an incorrect hand gesture that might be misconstrued as a political sign and result in me being arrested or, worse, 'disappeared'. I was not afraid that I had to scrape together what I needed just to survive until tomorrow. It was a new day, a new beginning, a chance to start a new life that had a bright future stretching ahead.

I was staying with friends from Zimbabwe, who were now living in London, for the first couple of months. My parents managed to send over boxes containing some of my essential belongings. I pounded the pavements in search of work, as it was now autumn and Christmas jobs were starting to be advertised.

I found a job working in a shop that sold kitchen wares – pots, pans, potato peelers, etc. While working there I was also applying for teaching jobs all over the country. I trusted God to lead me to where He wanted me to be.

After several interviews at a variety of schools, I was offered a job that was due to start in the New Year. I took it.

I moved and stayed with some relatives, also in London. I moved jobs too and found employment for December as a Christmas worker in the kitchen wares section of a popular department store on Oxford Street. This involved very early mornings – so early that the London Underground had only just opened when I got on the train, which felt like the middle of the night, and it was completely deserted, except for me, trying hard not to fall asleep or miss my stop.

It was New Year's Day 2004 and I was at work. The department store had offered triple pay as no one really wanted to go to work after partying the night before and, as I'd had no plans, that suited me fine. After work, I set off to my newly rented flat in Wisbech in north Cambridgeshire.

My mother's aunt, who had lived in the UK all her life, very kindly gave me a lift to the flat. She had filled the car with essentials she had spare. There was a camping bed, some bed linen and towels, cutlery and crockery as well as a couple of old pots and pans.

After we had unpacked the car, she took me along to a nearby supermarket and bought a whole load of groceries – it was extremely kind and generous of her.

The Christmas school holidays were not very long and it was only a day or two later that I was standing in front of my new class. I don't know who was more nervous, them or me.

I had a lot to learn, not just a different culture but also a whole new way of speaking. I found I had to change my vocabulary so that the children would understand me. I had to say 'trainers' for sports footwear instead of 'takkies', and 'jumper' for a pullover sweatshirt instead of 'jersey'.

The seasons were also back to front for me. I had always been used to a baking hot Christmas in the mid-summer heat of Zimbabwe. We would still celebrate it as close to the Victorian way as we could, complete with a big roast dinner, decorations and Christmas trees. We would often find someone dressed up as Father Christmas at one of the big shopping centres, with a red and white super-fluffy suit, the same as the ones in the UK. Shops would use white shoe-cleaning paint to make their windows look snowy, and we would send each other Christmas cards decorated with a little red-breasted robin standing in some snow, despite the fact that no one living in Zimbabwe had seen snow in their lives, nor a robin for that matter.

Along with the seasons was the difference in the school year. I had grown up with a school year that mirrored a calendar year. We started our new school year in January, just as we would the calendar year, but this was not how it was done in the UK. In the UK the school year started in September, as this was the term after the longest break over the summer months. This meant I found myself starting my teaching career in the UK partway through a school year.

Thankfully, the children in my class were wonderful. They made my first teaching experience in a new country a good one. We had lots of laughs and quite a bit of fun in the middle of a lot of hard work.

With my first full-time pay cheque I was able to pay back in full the friends who had lent me the money to pay off my bursary. My entire university education was paid for in one go (thanks to the devaluation of the Zimbabwean dollar).

Life had begun to stabilise.

As I was settling into the school, the headmaster asked to see me. He enquired as to what I had in the way of furniture in my flat, and I told him that I did not have very much. He then set about speaking to some of the staff as well as the school caretaker, whom he instructed to go around fetching bits of furniture and to also buy a new bed and mattress from a local shop. This was all delivered to my flat while I was at work one day. It made a big difference and was very welcome.

The headmaster asked me about what else I enjoyed or liked to do outside school time. I explained that I was looking for a lively church to attend. He then introduced me to a member of the teaching staff who was a Christian, and I was invited to go to visit his church in Wisbech.

So on Sunday I found my way to the community centre where the church held its meetings. It was just around the corner from my flat, which was convenient. Everyone at the church was friendly. Up at the front stood a few people clutching instruments – a couple of guitars, a keyboard and someone holding a microphone – a band. It looked promising.

However, when things got started, I was rather ambivalent about it. I wasn't being terribly inspired by anything that was going on. The songs being sung were so old, most of them had been written before I was born (or thereabouts). I thought the music was OK, but nothing earth-shattering. The Bible teaching was fair. I left with an open mind but decided that the next weekend I would try another church, in the nearby city of Peterborough.

So that is what I did. I had done a bit of research on the internet during the week to find out about the church I thought I would get along well with. Remember, these were the days when the internet was still very new. We still had to use a dial-up modem to connect and not many churches had websites, let alone kept the information they posted up to date. But I had found a church and I wanted to try it out to see if I felt 'at home' there.

On Sundays, the bus timetable was reduced, with fewer buses running. This meant that I had to catch a very early bus to get to Peterborough with enough time to walk to the venue before the service began. I arrived in the city centre on a dark, wet and cold February morning. The puddles on the pavement of the central square of the city still reflected the streetlights and neon shop signs as the sun began to claw its way up from its slumbers. I still had about two hours to wait before the service started. I wandered about looking for somewhere dry and warm where I could wait. After a bit of walking about I found a café.

I bought myself a cup of coffee and found the most comfortable seat I could. I sat and prayed and drank my coffee. I also had my Bible tucked in my backpack, so I pulled it out and started flipping the pages.

I found myself thinking about the church in Wisbech I had visited the week before. In my mind, I was listing all the things I would do differently if I were involved at that church. As soon as I had had that thought, I suddenly got a sense that God was speaking to me: 'Yes, and this is exactly why you are here.' He went on, 'I've not brought you here to *enjoy* church. I've brought you here to work and to serve. I have trained you and prepared you for this very task.'

It was at that moment I knew I had a direct calling from God to go back to the church in Wisbech and make it my home. But seeing as I was already in Peterborough, and by the time I had taken the bus journey back to Wisbech I would have missed church there anyway, I decided that for this week I would go ahead and visit the Peterborough church.

After waiting some more, I got the map out and navigated my way through the city to the venue where this church met. When I arrived, the place was deserted. I found a piece of paper stuck to the door saying that the church was not meeting there that weekend for some reason I can't remember now, and said where they were meeting instead. Well, I only knew how to get to this venue and had no idea where the other one was. Without smartphones or Google Maps to hand in those days, that was the end of my search. So I turned around and went back to Wisbech. This seemed to confirm that God didn't want me in Peterborough; He wanted me at that church in Wisbech. And that is what I did. I went back to The King's

Church, Wisbech, and have faithfully served there ever
since.

6
The Proposal

During my first few years in Wisbech, my mother and father were still living in Zimbabwe, and things were not getting any better; in fact, they were continuing to get worse.

I found a UK-based website where expat Zimbabweans could buy certain essentials using much-coveted foreign currency, and these were then collected by our relatives in Zimbabwe. We could buy things such as groceries, petrol and even satellite TV subscriptions. Once we had paid by credit card on the website, a code would be sent to the recipient's mobile phone in Zimbabwe. They were then instructed which shop or petrol station to go to where they could redeem their code. It was like a long-distance voucher system that bypassed the need for those living in Zimbabwe to obtain foreign currency and helped distant relatives to contribute in a very real way to the livelihoods of family still in the country.

I bought petrol rations for my mum and dad for many months this way. They later told me that without my assistance they would have been completely stranded, and with no shops within walking distance from where they lived, it was a lifeline.

As I was getting more and more settled in Wisbech, in 2007 I decided it was time to get on the property ladder. I moved out of the flat I had rented since I had first moved there and moved into a Victorian two-up-two-down mid-terrace house that I had managed to get a mortgage for. It was still within walking distance to work, so I was happy.

The time finally came in 2008 when Mum and Dad decided that the struggle to survive in Zimbabwe had come to an end. Things were bad and they were not coping well. So they packed a few boxes and shipped them over to me. A couple of weeks later, they too arrived in the UK.

My sister, Leigh, also left Zimbabwe at the same time as my parents, but she moved to neighbouring South Africa. She lived in the same town as my grandmother and uncle and aunt, so she had family nearby as well as a good network of friends that she built up for herself.

It was a good thing that I had just bought a house that could fit us all in, as my parents stayed with me for their first six months in the country. Mum got a teaching job at the same school as me, teaching the reception class. This enabled Mum and Dad to rent a place of their own in the town and life began to be more settled and secure for them.

A couple of years later, in 2010, the procedure was repeated, as my sister had decided to move from South Africa and join us in the UK. She also stayed with me for the first few months before finding a teaching job in Peterborough.

I was putting down roots in my local community. I was becoming increasingly involved in the local church, playing an instrument in the band and eventually leading it. Friendships were developing and I was getting to know lots of new people both in the church and among my work colleagues at school.

One particular family in the church, the Smiths, had taken me under their wing and would regularly invite me round for Sunday lunch and occasionally for an evening on a weekday as well.

As time went by, I found myself becoming more friendly with one of their daughters, Verity. Some years later, after forming a good friendship, we started dating. We were both Christians and believed strongly in the sanctity of marriage, so we both made the decision to keep the physical side of our relationship pure.

Sometime later I was walking on the beach at Wells-next-the-Sea in Norfolk with the rest of the Smith family. It was a cold day and the wind was bracing. We were wrapped up in winter coats. On the walk I quietly asked Verity's father if he would give me his daughter's hand in marriage. It was October and I had bought the engagement ring earlier that day and had it in my pocket. The plan was to propose during a big fireworks event we usually went to together on Bonfire Night on 5th November. The chat with her dad went very well and things were now ready for me to propose.

We stopped for fish and chips. I could hardly eat anything and went to the toilets. I was suddenly overcome with nervousness. My hands were shaking; my heart was racing. I knew that I couldn't wait until November to ask her to marry me. I had to do it now. Today.

After the fish and chips we were making our way back to the car park. We decided it would be fun to have a ride on the miniature railway. The seats were small and I had to duck my head to fit under the roof while sitting. Verity's sister is a doctor and she was sitting with other members of the family in the group of seats in front of us. The topic of conversation was about the worst-smelling things she had seen as a doctor. This meant everyone else was engrossed in conversation – I saw my opportunity. We were pretty much alone, being ignored anyway, so I took a deep breath and did it. I asked Verity to marry me.

I couldn't kneel down as the seats were too cramped. Verity didn't quite believe me at first, but soon figured out that I was being deadly serious. She said, 'Yes.'

For the rest of the train ride, we sat together, hand in hand, the only two people in the world who knew what had just happened between us. As soon as the train stopped, we told everyone else. She showed everyone the ring – it was official. We were engaged. There was much joy and merriment and we stopped off at a nice restaurant on the way home to celebrate.

In the summer of 2011, we were married. It was a lovely ceremony held in the church we could see from her parents' garden. Verity looked beautiful and I got choked up when I first saw her standing at the back of the church in her wedding dress as she prepared to walk down the aisle. The school choir came and sang, the church band led worship songs and, as requested, the preacher gave a good sermon that invited people to come to Jesus. It was very touching – even our photographer who was used to attending weddings all the time commented on her blog as to how moved she was by it.

Three years later, on a stormy afternoon, with lightning streaking across the sky, we were both ecstatic with joy as we welcomed our firstborn into the world. A daughter whom we called Katrina.

7
Even Through the Tears

Over the initial few months of first-time parenthood, it became apparent that kids need space – and lots of it; more for all the stuff that comes along with the addition of the extra small person in the household. We already knew that we wanted more than one child, and the space available in the Victorian mid-terrace was not sufficient. We needed to sell the house and buy a bigger one.

It was around Christmas-time in 2014. It's said that the best time of the year to sell property is just after Christmas, so we wanted everything ready for that date. We were optimistic that our house would sell fairly quickly. But we were wrong.

So began a year of having the house on the market. Trying to keep everything constantly tidy with a toddler is virtually impossible! We waited for the phone calls from the estate agents, which didn't happen very often, then swung into action, cleaning, hoovering and tidying the entire house. We endured the inspection of our home by strangers, who cast a judgemental eye over a place we loved. Then came the eternal wait to see if they might have put in an offer – or not. Excuses like the lack of off-road parking were reported back to us. We thought it unlikely anyone could find a Victorian mid-terraced house with off-road parking, as cars hadn't been invented when the houses were built! Anyway, we resigned ourselves to waiting – lowering the price a little – and waiting a bit more.

We had just welcomed 2016 together with family and friends and were optimistically looking to the excitement of the year ahead.

Early in the New Year, Verity began to suspect that she was pregnant. Sure enough, a pregnancy test revealed that she was. Before the pregnancy test was taken to confirm our suspicions, we knew that all was not well as Verity was experiencing sharp pain in her lower abdomen. In fact, this pain had prompted her to take the pregnancy test in the first place.

The pain came and went quite infrequently and irregularly but seemed to be getting stronger and longer each time it occurred until it reached the point where Verity couldn't move or think about anything else. She was also bleeding. Something was very wrong.

As soon as the test confirmed Verity was pregnant, we phoned family members to ask for prayer. Then we phoned 111 and explained the symptoms. We were given an out-of-hours appointment to see a doctor. Verity explained that she was pregnant and was experiencing pain, so he wanted to do another pregnancy test.

When she handed him the sample bottle, he was rather surprised and commented that there was blood.

Fighting the tears, Verity replied, 'I know!'

His test was also positive, so we were referred to the hospital.

This was a Saturday, and one when we had plans. I had organised a prophetic workshop[11] for the church band and celebration in the evening. A lot of time and planning had gone into it so we decided that Verity's mum would take her to the hospital, and if anything happened, I would then shoot over. If nothing happened, I would finish the meeting then come afterwards.

At the hospital there was lots of waiting around. Blood tests and more pregnancy tests were done. I arrived after the meeting and it was decided that an ultrasound was needed. One could be booked for Monday, but as I was working and had Fridays off we decided to wait until then.

When we were pregnant the first time round, my wife and I discovered that it is accepted in today's culture not to tell anyone about a pregnancy until after the first scan at three months. This is mainly because of the risk of complications, so no one will know if you have suffered a miscarriage if it were to happen in the early stages.

We decided right from the beginning that we would not do this. If we were pregnant, then we would let people know, regardless of the stage of pregnancy. We did not feel we should hide our pain if something were to go

---

[11] Prophecy is a spiritual gift (Romans 12:6) where people listen to what they believe the Holy Spirit is saying and then speak it out. This prophetic workshop was to help the band to be more open to the promptings of the Holy Spirit during times of sung worship and to learn how to be flexible and adapt their music or song to help facilitate the Holy Spirit's work within a church meeting. See also 1 Corinthians 14:1.

wrong. Now, I am not advocating that everyone should divulge their announcement of pregnancy immediately. This was a personal decision that seemed right for us.

On Sunday we told our church family that Verity was pregnant. The announcement was greeted with cheers that were quickly stifled as we went on to explain that there was something very wrong. We asked for prayer.

The week that followed went by in a bit of a daze. The anxiety and worry mixed with heartbreak were quite unbearable, even more so for Verity.

After what seemed like an eternity, Friday came. We went back to the hospital for the ultrasound.

We were called in and the scan began. After having done this before with our first child, we thought we knew what to expect. They use the scanner to look around the womb a bit, then they point the screen towards the parent/s so they can see the baby.

Time ticked by where all that could be heard was the sound of breathing. We were told that an internal scan was needed as the sonographer was struggling to find an image on the screen. This happened with our first child, so it was not a surprise, but was still a little disconcerting.

More time passed and the sonographer never pointed the screen towards us. Eventually she announced that she had finished and asked us to wait in the waiting room again.

Finally, we were called to see the lead midwife who told us that there was a pregnancy but it was ectopic. They would have to perform an operation to remove the embryo, which may mean the removal of the affected fallopian tube, where the embryo had incorrectly implanted itself, as well.

Throughout all their discussions with us, the hospital staff were very careful not to use the word 'baby' or anything that might make us think of this as anything other than a collection of malfunctioning cells.

It was already past lunchtime so we went and had something to eat in the hospital canteen. Of course, Verity did not feel very much like eating, which was just as well seeing as she was about to have an anaesthetic.

After lunch we went back to the ultrasound unit to wait to be escorted to the ward for surgery. While we were waiting, the sonographer said that there hadn't been a heartbeat. This caused Verity's emotions to come flooding out – this was the first time we were told that our baby was actually dead; it was also a relief. We felt that death had already happened and would not be caused by our decision for Verity to have the life-saving operation.

In the ward, Verity's pain escalated and she was given some morphine. Her dad had left work upon hearing the news and sat with Verity as I went home to pack her some overnight bags and arrange childcare for Katrina.

Before Verity was wheeled off in a hospital bed down the corridor wearing one of those flimsy hospital gowns that open at the back, we nervously gave each other a cuddle and a kiss. I said a silent prayer. Then I waited. I had a sermon to prepare so I found a comfortable spot and worked on it.

Sometime later, Verity was wheeled back into the ward. She had a damp towel on her head as she had started going into shock after the operation. She was conscious although still very groggy from the anaesthetic. As soon as she saw me, she burst into tears, saying over and over, 'Our baby died! Our baby died!'

We had lost our precious baby but had saved Verity's life. We were so thankful that there were no signs of life when Verity had had the scan. Our little one had already died before the operation.

Most people have differing opinions as to when life begins. For many, our ectopic pregnancy was just a collection of stem cells multiplying in the wrong place. We had no doubt that in those cells there was life, the life of our child. A beautiful spirit created by God. We knew that they did not just disappear into the ether but one day, once we too have stepped into eternity, we will get to meet that person, knowing that they are our child.

All through the process, we kept our church family updated with the news. Not because we wanted sympathy, but because we recognised that we were walking this journey of faith together through the good and the bad.

Both my wife and I held leadership positions within the church. It would have been all too easy to hide behind the mask of, 'I'm a church leader – so of course my life is brilliant!' No! We recognised that leaders should share their humanity, their vulnerability and their pain with those whom they lead. If we were not prepared to model the behaviour we were expecting from those we led, we weren't going to achieve the results we were hoping for. Sharing something personal and painful clothed in humility and vulnerability was part of the package for an authentic leader, not a sign of weakness.

As a result of going against the cultural norm of keeping quiet about Verity's early pregnancy and miscarriage, we believed we helped others in our church to see how being more open in times of hurt and grief could be such an amazingly healthy thing to do. We were so supported, upheld in prayer, and had many offers of practical support too during that difficult time.

This is an extract of something I wrote on my blog at this time:

> 30th January 2016
> We are the church, called to love one another. If no one knows you are hurting (yes, even if you are a church leader) no one will be able to help you.
> So be encouraged. Share one another's burdens. Let people in on times of grief and loss and experience the freedom and liberation that comes, even through the tears!

I preached my sermon at church and then immediately made my way over to the hospital to be by Verity's side. While I was at the hospital trying to navigate all the emotions of grief as well as trying to support my wife, my phone rang. It was the estate agent. I was all ready to put them off and say that we would not be available for a viewing for the next few weeks, when he announced that he had received an offer for our house! We were overjoyed. This was a silver lining to a very dark cloud.

We had waited more than a year to reach this point, so after a couple of weeks to allow Verity to recover and for us to come to terms with what had happened, we started house hunting.

It was quite a task to agree on a property, but both Verity and I fell in love with a fantastic four-bedroom detached house that was perfect for us. We put an offer in and it was accepted.

So began the long and tedious legal process of buying and selling a house. But we were happy that things were happening and were very pleased about the new house. It would be worth the wait.

Around February time, while showering, I noticed a mysterious lump in my left armpit. It was about the size of a large marble. I thought it was a bit strange and stopped my mind from leaping to the worst possible conclusion, as I have the habit of doing. The armpit is one of the places in the body where we have glands, and these often get enlarged from time to time when we have a cold or are fighting off an infection. I dismissed it. I thought if it was still around in a few weeks, then I would tell Verity, as I didn't want to worry her unnecessarily.

My mind was focused on other things.

Having only just lost our unborn child, the pain was still very raw and visceral. Both Verity and I felt that we were under spiritual attack. Now, please do not misunderstand – not every setback, criticism or hardship in life is a spiritual attack, but there are times when it happens, and it is important to recognise where the battle is truly being fought:

> Be strong in the Lord and in his mighty power.
> Put on the full armour of God, so that you can
> take your stand against the devil's schemes. For

our struggle is not against flesh and blood, but against the rulers, against the authorities, against the powers of this dark world and against the spiritual forces of evil in the heavenly realms. Therefore put on the full armour of God, so that when the day of evil comes, you may be able to stand your ground, and after you have done everything, to stand.
(Ephesians 6:10-13)

This was one of those times. Many big, significant things had gone wrong and continued to do so. Pressures had increased dramatically in all spheres of life, enough to push us to breaking point, and it seemed there was no escape. Stress levels were high and emotions were fraying.

At times like this it was quite common for us to receive encouraging words from well-meaning Christian friends. Some pieces of advice were more helpful and more welcomed than others. For example, quite a few people told us that God would not give us anything more than we could cope with. Yet here we were, not coping. So how could this be true? I took a closer look at what the Bible actually says in 1 Corinthians 10:13:

No temptation has overtaken you except what is common to mankind. And God is faithful; he will not let you be tempted beyond what you can bear. But when you are tempted, he will also provide a way out so that you can endure it.

I discovered that quite often this scripture is taken out of context as it specifically refers to times of temptation, not suffering.[12]

In fact, I believe that God allows times of suffering that are deliberately beyond what we can possibly cope with on our own. We need to reach a point where we realise that there is no way out through our own effort. We need to turn to Jesus and shout, 'Help!' We are brought to the end of ourselves so that we can find ourselves safe in the arms of Jesus and know that there is no other way through except for throwing ourselves into His 'everlasting arms' (Deuteronomy 33:27). When we acknowledge our weakness, it is here that we find our true strength – and it doesn't come from us.

Even in the middle of this trying time, God was still very much in the picture. There was good news punctuating the bad. Light was breaking through the darkness from time to time that let us know that God was still in control and that He was at work in every situation, even the bad ones, for our good according to His will.[13]

My father-in-law gave me some sound advice. He said that when we were under attack, God was allowing it so that we would draw closer to Him.

> We are hard pressed on every side, but not crushed; perplexed, but not in despair; persecuted, but not abandoned; struck down, but not destroyed. We always carry around in

---

[12] Adapted from an idea by Patrick Regan and Liza Hoeksma, *When Faith Gets Shaken* (Oxford: Monarch Books, 2015), pp148-149. Used by permission.
[13] Romans 8:28.

our body the death of Jesus, so that the life of Jesus may also be revealed in our body. For we who are alive are always being given over to death for Jesus' sake, so that his life may also be revealed in our mortal body. So then, death is at work in us, but life is at work in you.
(2 Corinthians 4:8-12)

I was mindful of my father-in-law's words and tried to draw near to God during that time, even when it felt as if I was dragging my heart along a harsh gravel road with each grief-filled step. I knew that although I may be 'hard pressed on every side' – I was 'not crushed'! Jesus was my hope – a hope that could never be overcome, no matter how dark or how hard the road seemed.

8
Lumps and Bumps

The streets of York were cold and wet. I was tired, having had little sleep the night before. I was in the middle of a school residential trip in early March 2016 in my role as schoolteacher, accompanying around thirty eleven-year-olds on this educational visit. We were on the steps that led up to the side of York Minster, probably having a sandwich or waiting for a tour guide, I can't quite remember.

My phone rang. It was the estate agent. It wasn't good news. After around a month of going through the legal process of selling our house and buying a new one, the person who wanted to buy our house had pulled out of the agreement. The sale had fallen through. This in turn meant that we could no longer proceed with buying the house we had set our hearts on, and that sale fell through as well.

The news came as a blow. We felt as if we were entering a downward, uncontrollable spiral. But I was still able to take a deep breath and soldier on. I told myself, 'You've got to keep going.' It had taken more than a year to reach this point in the sale of the house. We would just have to brace ourselves, keep calm and carry on.

Our house was put back on the market.

Around this time, my wife and I were chatting with some friends about our situation. We were discussing the sale of our house falling through and the ectopic pregnancy as well as God's faithfulness. We were talking about our recent pain and hardships, and I wasn't being particularly optimistic, I must admit, but someone commented that I needed to have more faith, and everything would work out.

Now at first glance, this makes sense. God calls us to 'live by faith, not by sight' (2 Corinthians 5:7); 'And without faith it is impossible to please God, because anyone who comes to him must believe that he exists and that he rewards those who earnestly seek him' (Hebrews 11:6). However, the error is in the belief that faith is an end in itself. That by simply having more of this thing called *faith* we can somehow magically achieve everything we ever wanted and life will suddenly turn around for the better.

Faith is meant to be a connector, a way for us to relate to Jesus. Faith needs to be *in* someone or something. I think of it as a Wi-Fi signal, a means of connection. You can install multiple broadband boxes in your house to get more and more Wi-Fi signal, but without a website to visit or an email account to check, you can have as much signal as you like but it will not do anything for you. Faith is a connector, not a destination.

'Now faith is confidence in what we hope for and assurance about what we do not see' (Hebrews 11:1). This is one of the central verses that has helped me understand what faith is. Here is how *The Message* says it:

> The fundamental fact of existence is that this trust in God, this faith, is the firm foundation under everything that makes life worth living. It's our handle on what we can't see. The act of faith is what distinguished our ancestors, set them above the crowd.
> (Hebrews 11:1-2)

Notice how our understanding of faith and its purpose should be found *in* and *through* God.

In his book *Preaching*, Timothy Keller encourages us to view everything in the Bible through the lens of the gospel, through the saving grace of Jesus. The basic premise is that all Scripture points towards the central event of the cross in one way or another.[14] So, for example, James 1:6, which says, 'But when you ask, you must believe and not doubt, because the one who doubts is like a wave of the sea, blown and tossed by the wind.' This should not be viewed as a cosmic summoning of faith in our own strength to gain blessings and an improvement of life's circumstances. Rather, it is encouraging us to believe and not doubt Jesus! We should not doubt Jesus' power, His sovereignty, His good and perfect will in every situation. When we doubt, we are to look to Jesus, not to ourselves and our feeble faith-summoning abilities.

We also see Jesus accusing His disciples of having 'little faith' when they are afraid and caught up in a storm at sea

---

[14] Adapted from an idea by Timothy Keller, *Preaching* (London: Hodder & Stoughton Ltd, 2015), pp47-69.

(Matthew 8:23-27). Was this because their faith was small and they had neglected to go to the spiritual gym to 'work out' their faith muscles enough? Or was it because in their fear, their attention and focus moved away from Jesus and on to the raging waves and blowing winds around them? I believe it is the latter. Refocusing on Jesus is indeed what saved them from the storm. Jesus calmed the sea and the storm stopped. They did not need to summon up reserves of faith or try harder to have more faith. They had to refocus their attention back on Jesus and trust in Him to rescue them.

Jesus is 'the pioneer and perfecter' of our faith (Hebrews 12:2). We are to look to Him and dig deeper into His presence when we need to exercise faith in uncertain times.

Even in the middle of those painful events, Verity and I were confident that God was in control as we daily surrendered our will to His, trusting by faith that His plans were bigger and better than ours; that we were safe in the loving arms of our Saviour.

It was now mid-March 2016. The mysterious armpit lump had not gone away. I summoned up the courage to casually mention it to Verity. She was obviously worried and insisted that I make an appointment to go to see the GP straight away. I did so the next day.

The GP poked and prodded me.

'So how long ago did you notice this lump?'

'About a month ago,' I replied.

'Have you noticed it get any bigger or smaller or change shape in any way?'

'No.'

'Has it been causing you any pain or discomfort?'

'No, it hasn't. I'm really only aware of it when I'm showering. I don't feel it otherwise.'

He prodded other areas of my body.

'What we will do is we will keep an eye on it for now. I'm sure it's nothing to worry about. The chances that it is something more sinister are very slim indeed. But I do want you to come back in a couple of weeks to see if there have been any changes or not.'

We were scheduled to go on a family holiday to Cape Town, South Africa, at the end of March, so an appointment was made for me to see him again as soon as I got back in mid-April.

9
Worst Fears Confirmed

After a very long flight we finally touched down at London's Heathrow Airport. Our South African holiday had come to an end and we were daring to be optimistic as to what God had in store for the next chapter of our lives. We felt rested and rejuvenated. Our grief was starting to be punctuated by healing and peace. The raw, open, emotional wound had started to scab over.

Shortly after we got back, I returned to the GP. There had been no change in the status of the lump in my armpit.

The doctor had another brief look and decided that as nothing had changed, he would refer me to a consultant at the nearby hospital in the town of King's Lynn.

'I'm sure it's nothing to worry about,' he explained, 'but we don't like to take any chances with lumps. So it is best to get it checked out.'

I was grateful that further investigation was going to happen, and I was still fairly optimistic, though some anxious thoughts did start to creep in. I remember telling a colleague at work that I had found a lump and I was a bit worried as I was having further tests. They were encouraging and supportive, which helped.

Soon after that GP visit, I was packing bags and guitars, loading up books and CDs, checking postcodes for the SatNav and putting petrol in the car for an event I had been booked to play guitar and sing at called The Pursuit. This was a sixty-hour non-stop worship festival. It was happening just outside London over the long Bank Holiday weekend in early May. I was scheduled to play an early morning slot from 3am to 5am on the Sunday.

On the morning I was due to drive to London, an appointment had been made for me to see a consultant at the nearby hospital in King's Lynn. Verity came along to the hospital with me.

The consultant seemed tired, and her manner was quite stern and to the point. She had a look at the lump in my armpit, then asked if she could examine elsewhere.

She felt my other armpit, my groin, and prodded around my abdomen and neck a bit too. While she was doing this, she was silent. Then she asked, 'So have you noticed all these other lumps, then?' My stomach turned. I couldn't quite believe what I was hearing. More lumps? Surely not!

I told her that I had not noticed them. I asked her to point them out to me as I couldn't quite believe it. I couldn't really feel anything particularly different.

Anyway, she could not say what the lumps were at that stage without taking a biopsy. So that was booked for a week's time.

Verity and I were both quite shaken by this visit. We didn't really say much in the car on the journey home, our minds jumping to all sorts of possible conclusions, none of which was particularly pleasant.

We both decided that I would continue with my weekend plans and go to The Pursuit that afternoon. Besides, I was feeling fine (as I had done up until then).

The weekend took on a different focus for me from that point. Instead of me going to minster to others (which I still did), it proved to be a valuable time where I could just crumble and collapse in God's presence to try to make sense of it all. There was no indication of what we were dealing with at this point, just that it could be cancer, and in my mind, this meant a very strong possibility that I could die.

The times of singing were immensely powerful and often saw me in a heap curled up on the floor of the tent, sobbing and crying out to God for healing – for life – for salvation from death! Sometimes the words would choke me, and I couldn't speak at all. I had to take extra water bottles into the tent to keep me hydrated as I was crying so much.

During this time, I got the sense that God was giving me strength as I waited on Him. He showed me a few things: I had already given Him my life, so my body belonged to Him too; it was part of the package! So ultimately it was up to Him if He healed me or not. It was out of my control. I was, and am, in His hands, and I was safe there, no matter what happened.

I also came face to face with the idea of dying. It was in God's presence that I discovered I was actually not that afraid of death. If He were to call me home, I would go willingly and gladly. However, this did leave a lot of other things that hurt. Such as, I was a young guy (I know that is a matter of opinion – but I was only thirty-six at the time) and I didn't believe God had finished with me yet. There was still more for me to do for Him on this earth. There was the pain of missing seeing my child grow up; to see her lose her first tooth or to be there on her first day of school. Thoughts of missing a chance to possibly walk her down the aisle or maybe even hold a grandchild of my own one day went through my mind. I was sad about all the hopes and dreams I still had that might never be realised. I felt the pain of the possible separation from my wife and felt guilty that I might leave her to cope with everything on her own. All this really hurt.

I was also prompted to finish some of the things I had started. For example, a book I had almost finished writing but had neglected for a few years. A couple of new songs I needed to make demos of and put up on the internet. Time was precious and time was short. Procrastination was not helpful. I also got a sense during one of the sermons that God was going to use this time to accelerate things for me and my ministry, to move things along at a supernatural speed. The time had come.

On the last morning of The Pursuit I believe God told me my diagnosis.

During the last meeting, there was a spontaneous prophetic song[15] and, in a funny twist of events, the words from a popular children's book were sung. It tells a story of a family who are going exploring and encounter various obstacles along the way. They realise that they cannot

---

[15] A song that is sung spontaneously without rehearsal or being previously written down. It is usually believed that the person singing this type of song is hearing directly from the Holy Spirit and is singing what they are sensing He is saying.

avoid the obstacles but have to endure them by going through them as the only way of getting to the other side.

Through this, I believe God was communicating with me and was confirming my fears – that I indeed had cancer and I would just have to hold tightly on to Him to get through it. But get through it I would! I was going on my own adventure. I was certain that it was going to be full of hardship, pain and risk but hopeful that the 'eternal glory' would far outweigh the temporary suffering I may experience (2 Corinthians 4:17).

We so often pray that we be delivered *from* a situation, and God sometimes does deliver us this way. However, sometimes we are delivered *through* a trial. And it is as we go through it we find Jesus, our friend, companion and guide – the 'man of sorrows' (Isaiah 53:3, NLT) who knows what it is to suffer – walking each step of the journey with us, holding us and helping us until we get to the other side.

The Bible calls those who believe in Jesus, overcomers (1 John 5:4-5). This clearly indicates that there must be something to overcome. Life does not suddenly become free from pain or suffering when we choose to follow Jesus. If this were true and life contained no trials, there would be no reason for our faith.[16]

I wrote on my blog, recalling what had happened at The Pursuit:

> The main thing that I have come to realise is that God is with me no matter what life may bring.

---

[16] Adapted from Brian Houston, *Live, Love, Lead* (London: Hodder & Stoughton Ltd, 2015), p200.

God is with me and God is in control. God is
bigger than my fears. God is stronger than
cancer. God is God and if He is for me, then who
can be against me?[17] I trust God for healing. I
trust God for victory, but I do not presume to
know His plan. Even if I die, God is good and
God is in control. God is on the throne!

Once I had realised this, God filled me with such an inner
peace that many people mistook it for bravery or courage.

Bible teacher and author Timothy Keller puts it like
this:

Christian peace does not start with the ousting of
negative thinking. If you do that, you may
simply be refusing to face how bad things are.
That is one way to calm yourself – by refusing to
admit the facts. But it will be short-lived peace!
Christian peace doesn't start that way. It is not
that you stop facing the facts, but you get a living
power that comes into your life and enables you
to face those realities, something that lifts you up
over and through them.[18]

I see it as surrender.

I was weak. I was not strong. But Jesus was. He was my
strength. He was my source. He was my everything – He
had to be because there was no way that I could face this
on my own.

---

[17] See Romans 8:31.
[18] Timothy Keller, *Walking with God Through Pain and Suffering*
(London: Hodder & Stoughton Ltd, 2013), p297. Used by permission.

But he said to me, 'My grace is sufficient for you, for my power is made perfect in weakness.' Therefore I will boast all the more gladly about my weaknesses, so that Christ's power may rest on me. That is why, for Christ's sake, I delight in weaknesses, in insults, in hardships, in persecutions, in difficulties. For when I am weak, then I am strong.

(2 Corinthians 12:9-10)

There were times during my journey when things felt surreal or extremely uncomfortable and embarrassing.

My biopsy appointment had arrived. It had been booked in the brand-new Breast Care Unit of the Queen Elizabeth Hospital in King's Lynn. As it was explained to me, the unit was the only one that had the necessary equipment to do a biopsy of the lump in my armpit.

The look on the receptionist's face when I arrived at the Breast Care Unit was priceless. She looked at my appointment letter, clicked away on the computer for a bit, then looked at the letter again. She was obviously not used to booking a male in for a biopsy in this section of the hospital and I had taken her by surprise.

The doctor who performed the biopsy was quite the opposite. She took everything in her stride and set us immediately at ease with her friendly and encouraging manner. She was trying to reassure us that it could still be nothing, and even if it was something, the type of cancer it was likely to be was a highly survivable type.

I looked away as the enormous biopsy needle appeared. I heard a few loud clicks and felt some pressure in my armpit. Then it was all over. Not bad, really.

We were told we could expect the results within the week. I believed I knew the diagnosis and had already started to come to terms with it, but would still be happy to get it confirmed.

A few days later, Verity told me she thought she might be pregnant again. Off to the supermarket we went to buy a pregnancy test. We did not have to wait long before we learned that we were going to be welcoming another child into our family.

About a week after the biopsy, we were back at the hospital to see the original consultant – the stern one – to get the results. We sat down and she explained that they had found that I had non-Hodgkin lymphoma. We knew this was serious news but no one actually said the word 'cancer'.

Verity bravely asked, 'So it is cancer, then?'

'Yes, it is,' came the reply.

This hit Verity hard. I too was a bit taken aback, although I knew who was in control and was holding me tightly at that moment. The rest of the brief appointment went by in a bit of a blur.

I had to ask the consultant to repeat the type of cancer a few times as I tried to take it in – non-Hodgkin lymphoma. In the end, a nurse wrote it down on a piece of paper for us to take with us, warning us not to Google it as there was so much misinformation on the internet.

They explained it was what they call a 'slow-grower' so I had in fact had it for years without knowing it! But this also meant that treatment was unlikely to be needed for many years. For now, they were adopting a 'wait-and-see' approach. Owing to the way the NHS is funded, if a condition is not life-threatening, treatment is delayed until it is. They would monitor the cancer until it reached a point at which it was dangerous.

A CT scan was booked for the doctors to get a good look at my lymphatic system so that the monitoring could begin.

We both stumbled out of the hospital and Verity needed to sit down for a while on a nearby bench. We hugged and had a few tears, then took a deep breath and continued on our way home, where we broke the news to family.

10
The 'C' Word

Continuing in the vein of being open and honest with our lives and being vulnerable with those we led in church, the following Sunday Verity and I let people know our latest news. We were delighted to be expecting our second child, especially given the added complication that this could happen at all after the recent ectopic pregnancy. Yet our joy was mixed with fear and uncertainty, as I had just had the devastating news that I had been diagnosed with cancer.

This period was bittersweet for us. We held on to these two things: that through *all* things Jesus will be glorified and that He can turn *all* things 'for the good of those who love him'. (Romans 8:28).

It was at this point I began to feel the significance of the blog I wrote; I believed that God wanted me to use my experience to help others by simply sharing my journey.

Some friends got in touch to say they saw two miracles in the making: the birth of our child and me becoming cancer-free. My friends saw the birth of my child as a miracle in the sense that any child is a miracle, but actually, this particular child was more of a miracle than they might have thought as in retrospect we worked out that she was conceived at the last possible moment it was possible before my chemotherapy began.

This was what we started praying for. As it turned out, friends, family and complete strangers from all over the world started to get in touch to say that they were praying too. I felt comforted and supported and could let go of the situation a bit more and rest in Jesus' loving arms.

I certainly didn't want my blog to become a depressing chronicle of my life, but if I truly felt it was important for Christian leaders to model humility and authenticity, even if it meant people getting to see them at their lowest point and in their most pain, then I had to do what I believed. I had to walk the walk and not just talk the talk.

As well as the blog, I spoke quite openly with people about my cancer and my treatments. This generated a rather strange response from some people. The response I am referring to is when the mention of 'cancer' is omitted from the conversation completely, even though it is what is being spoken about. Or it is referred to in hushed tones as 'the C word'. It is almost as if people sometimes fear to speak its name.

I was a little afraid of the unknown possibilities of my treatment. But mostly I was sad. Sad at the possibility that death might separate me from those I loved most dearly. However, there was joy in the pain. There was hope in the tears.

Waking up in the morning was rather an ordeal for the days and months after receiving my diagnosis. During the first few seconds of waking up I had forgotten the bad news, then as my mind became more fully conscious and alert, the realisation of 'I have cancer' came rushing into my mind. This left both my wife and me with a sense that we were no longer safe – we were now treading on a very unfamiliar and potentially lethal pathway. One we could not avoid.

I was not afraid of death. I was not afraid of cancer. I knew Jesus was in control. All I had to do was rest in Him and His peace:

> So do not fear, for I am with you;
> do not be dismayed, for I am your God.
> I will strengthen you and help you;
> I will uphold you with my righteous right hand.
> (Isaiah 41:10)

In mid-May 2016 I had my first CT scan. I managed to navigate my way around the hospital's corridors and find the department where I was supposed to be. There were yellow signs on some of the doors warning of 'radiation'. They were a bit stark and cold and not particularly comforting.

I had never had a CT scan before, so I had no idea what to expect.

I removed all metal objects from my pockets – keys, mobile phone, a watch, my belt with its buckle. I placed them on a nearby chair in the CT scan room.

A friendly nurse explained what would happen. I was not expecting an injection, let alone a cannula. But a cannula is what I got. It was fitted into the centre of my left arm and a tube attached it to a drip. I then lay on a tray that moved in and out of the ring of the CT machine, which looked like a large mechanical doughnut. The nurse disappeared behind a protective screen where the controls were. He spoke to me through a speaker and let me know when he was about to administer the injection via remote control. The injection contained a dye that would help the machine have a look at my insides. I had to lie very still and hold my breath for a while when the machine told me to do so.

Then he released the dye. It gave me a metallic taste in my mouth, and I felt a warm sensation sweep over my entire body as it spread through my system.

It was soon over, and I was told that I could expect the results in six to eight weeks.

Three days after the CT scan, we received the good news that we had sold the house again. We had put it back on the market after the initial sale had fallen through. Our first reaction to the news was to phone the estate agent to see if the house we had set our hearts on was still available. It too had just had a sale fall through so was only just back on the market, but at a more expensive price than we had originally offered. However, with my life insurance company having agreed to pay out on my claim, as I had critical illness cover, we could afford it. So the legal process of selling and buying houses began all over again.

Life continued as normally as it could. We were in the 'wait-and-see' stage and I was trying to get my head around living life with cancer. Physically I felt absolutely fine, as I always had done. Verity was in the throes of dealing with first-trimester morning sickness.

I was sitting at my desk on a Monday afternoon, just settling down to marking some maths books while my class were outside doing sports, a rare moment of stillness and calm in an otherwise highly stressful environment, when my mobile phone rang.

It was my wife, who was having a day out with Katrina. She explained that the doctor had been trying to get hold of me all day and couldn't so in the end he had phoned her instead.

The instruction was simple: pack a bag and get to the hospital now! This was unexpected and frightening as we were anticipating the results in six to eight weeks, not one week later.

I rushed downstairs, leaving a pile of half-marked books, explained to the head teacher what was happening and then I was gone. Little did I know that I would not set foot inside the school again for several months.

Verity was already back from her day trip. We packed an overnight bag and headed for the hospital in King's Lynn.

When we arrived, I saw a specialist who would look after me for the coming months and years. He explained that they had looked at my CT scan results and, apart from lots of small lumps in my armpits, neck and groin areas, they had found a very large mass in my abdomen. It measured 14cm by 8cm and was equivalent in size to a 14oz/400ml takeaway coffee cup. It was pressing on my left kidney and they needed to operate straightaway. This meant that I had Stage Four cancer (the highest and severest stage you can get) and needed to begin treatment immediately.

He explained to me that if they did not operate now to add a stent to support my kidney while they treated the cancer, it was extremely likely I would be in renal failure within a couple of weeks. He was most surprised when I told him that I felt completely well and that I was not experiencing any pain whatsoever.

They took me straight to a bed in the Shouldham oncology ward and started to treat the tumours at once. They hooked me up to an intravenous drip and gave me about forty steroid tablets to swallow. Talk about taking a whole box of pills at once! This was to start the process of shrinking the tumours as quickly as they could.

The following day I had the operation that inserted a stent into my left kidney duct to save it.

This left me with a dull ache, and going to the toilet was very uncomfortable for a while, mainly owing to the entry point they had used to insert the stent without the need for a scalpel.

A nurse came and spoke to my wife and me about a number of things, including how my diet and temperature should be carefully monitored while having chemotherapy. If my temperature were to go above 37.5°C, I was to call a hotline number immediately and would be admitted to hospital straight away. My diet had to avoid all sorts of potentially harmful things – no takeaways, no raw or partially cooked eggs, no leftovers (everything had to be fresh and free from possible bacterial contamination). Verity commented that it was very similar to the advice that she had just been given as a pregnant mother.

We spoke about banking sperm, as a very possible side effect of chemotherapy was infertility. Arrangements were made for this to be done at a fertility clinic before I began the treatment.

We also spoke about faith. We explained we were Christians and what we believed God was showing us at the time. The nurse said that in her experience she had found those with faith tend to cope with things a lot better in times like this.

The following day I was wheeled across the hospital to the pregnancy scanning unit. Whenever I was in hospital they didn't allow me to walk anywhere; I had to sit in a wheelchair and be pushed by a porter.

When the porter got to the door of the unit, he knocked. A nurse opened it. She looked very surprised and said, 'We don't scan men here! You've brought him to the wrong place.' I then explained that I was there to be with my wife who was due to have an early scan (owing to the ectopic pregnancy she'd had before). She hadn't arrived yet. I was allowed in.

It was wonderful to be able to see the peanut shape on the screen of the ultrasound machine, which had a tiny flicker of a heartbeat thumping away inside it.

The nurse was very happy with the baby's placement and development. We left with big smiles on our faces, although I was wheeled back to my hospital bed.

A few days later my kidney function had improved enough for me to be allowed to return home. I left armed with a carrier bag full of pills, syringes and a sharps bin.

Before they gave me the medicines, a nurse came to see me to show me how to inject myself in the stomach, near to my belly button. This daily injection was to help thin my blood, as they were concerned the tumour in my abdomen would cause blood clots.

I really didn't like self-injecting into my stomach. The injection was hit-and-miss in terms of pain. If I got the needle in the right spot, it wouldn't hurt going in, but if I got it on a nerve – ouch! Besides the initial injection hurting or not, my belly would ache badly for about half an hour afterwards. Injecting myself was also quite a big psychological hurdle I had to overcome; I had to take several deep breaths before plunging the needle in. And so began a daily ritual that would continue for the next six months.

When I got home, I also unpacked the yellow sharps bin they had given me to dispose of all the single-use syringes and needles safely. This was a moment of disaster. I had never encountered one before, and as I got it out of its box I noticed that a little plastic slidey thingy on the top was ajar. So I decided to shut it until I needed to put something in it.

Click.

Only then did I realise I had accidentally closed it permanently and there was no budging it (believe me, I tried). Off I went in search of a replacement that I had to buy from a local pharmacy. What a waste.

The end of May was approaching. Verity and I found ourselves journeying along green country lanes heading towards Cambridge. We arrived at a very posh manor house that had been converted into a swish fertility clinic. This was to be a very surreal experience, to say the least.

An hour of form-filling later and I was presented with a small plastic pot and escorted to a very clinical room where I was to perform my duty and leave a deposit in the pot while following all sorts of clinical rules and procedures. It was hardly a romantic or natural setting for such a thing. It wasn't easy, but I got the job done.

We were still not too sure what we thought about artificial insemination or in vitro fertilisation and where that left us in relation to our faith and ethics, but time was short. Chemotherapy was going to begin any day now. We decided to get a sample stored while we could and we would deal with the dilemmas it presented at a later date. Hopefully, the possibility of future children remained open to us if the chemotherapy did affect my fertility.

Since letting everyone know my diagnosis, and as I kept them up to date with the various stages of my treatment and the problems with the house sale, I was blessed as I continued to receive messages of support from friends, family and strangers from all over the world.

It is at times like this, when things are tough and death is a real possibility, that the foundations of one's life are exposed. Indeed, the foundations of the lives of those around us are also laid bare – family and friends who want to offer some comfort and express the depth of their emotion, as well as to lend support and encouragement.

From my point of view, this was quite touching. I was at peace, but there were others around me who were not. There were times when I found myself smiling inwardly as I talked or listened to others and then found myself offering them the comfort and support they were trying to extend towards me.

At other times, I felt enfolded and held up by the prayers various people from all over the world told me they were saying on my behalf.

I was also touched by other offers of support where friends without faith sent me 'good wishes' or 'positive vibes'. Although I did not really connect as deeply with these sentiments, I could see their heart and their desire to bless. At such times, when death knocks on your door, there is a natural desire to attempt to try to connect with the spiritual, yet their experience of such things was limited. I just hoped that as they journeyed with me they would be able to catch a glimpse of the eternal hope I had in Jesus.

11
From the Outside Looking In

As I faced up to this battle with cancer, I acknowledged that it affected not only me but those around me too. Below are some thoughts from my darling wife, Verity, and her reflections on our shared journey up until this point:

30th May 2016

I just read Matt's blog about him dealing with the prospect of having cancer and him coming to terms with it all, and it made me realise that I really haven't come to terms with it. My mind at the moment seems a lot messier and more turbulent.

We first properly suspected it might be serious after he saw the consultant and she found more lumps all over. It wasn't just a case of a simple cyst. He then went away for the weekend and surrounded himself with God and came back with a real peace and acceptance. I, on the other hand, spent this weekend without him trying desperately not to think at every point in the day what my life would be like if he died.

I've noticed that people have different ways of coping with worry and lots of people seem to try to ignore the worst-case scenario and choose to focus on the best case. I am not like that; I am the opposite. I must really try not to dwell purely on the worst that could happen. I think you actually need a bit of both as I don't think it's good to live in denial and then be shocked and crushed if the worst were to happen, but neither should you live by fear and lose the joy of today by focusing on 'what if'.

Anyway, I do think about what if Matt dies and, unfortunately, I do not yet have the peace that he has. The thought makes me feel sick. Every morning I have been waking up with a feeling of unease, of disquiet, as if I am not safe. And then I remember why. I could lose my husband. The person who shares my life and is supposed to be with me through it all. I remember how nervous I was throughout most of our engagement, worrying about whether this was the right thing to do and what if something went wrong. Ever since our wedding day I have had no doubts that this was what God had planned and that we can get through anything together. Don't get me wrong, our marriage is not perfect, but I know that it was the right thing to do and it brings a lot more blessing than if we had stayed apart.

But marriage is supposed to be for life, for a long life. You grow old together and then, when you are in your seventies or older, you must face the coming separation. It's not supposed to be finished when you've only just begun. We're just coming up to our fifth anniversary and I'm finding it so hard to face the fact that I may be married for less than ten years and then be without him. I fear that

I will live the rest of my life in the pain that I have lost the love of my life.

So many women I have met are proud, strong and independent and are more than happy to admit it. I, on the other hand, am an extremely dependent person. I went through a time of being extremely nervous about going out of the house. I used to get nervous about the shopping if Matt wasn't coming with me. I honestly do not know how or if I would cope with living alone. But of course, I have a daughter. Even when I feel hopeless, God brings light.

This situation has shown me that my dependency is no longer on Matt but actually is where it should be; I am totally dependent on God. I don't feel like my life will be destroyed if Matt dies, even though it will hurt more than anything I can imagine. I know God will get me through it. I am dependent on God because I have to be. He is the only thing that is safe and secure, and He is always faithful and never grows weary of me.

The thing is – I do not have to rely on my own strength and understanding. I know that God has my life in His hands and that He has good plans for me,[19] although it doesn't feel like that at the moment. Actually, it's not about how I feel, because I feel scared and overwhelmed and like my life would be nothing but misery if Matt were to die. What I have to rely on is what I know of God. And I know God is good. I know that he can use all things 'for the good of those who love him'.[20] I know He loves me, and Matt and our children (even the unborn ones). I know

[19] See Jeremiah 29:11.
[20] Romans 8:28.

that God is already using this situation to draw us closer to Him and is speaking to others through us and the situation. I have never been so thankful to know Jesus. There is no way I would get through this without Him. And I have never felt so surrounded by love from the people around us; I'm so thankful for the family that is church.

So maybe I do have some peace; I know my Father is the one in control. But that doesn't stop my mind being turbulent, picturing watching Matt die; picturing our children growing up without their daddy; imagining living in pain for the rest of my life. And now we're expecting another child and looking at buying a bigger house, and I think of a year's time with the four of us being together in our lovely new home and I can barely breathe because I know this is what I've got to lose.

I know God can heal and I believe that He will, but I'm terrified that He might not. Even if the worst were to happen I know He would use it to bring glory to His name. At times like this God can often seem to be quiet and distant; it's just part and parcel of the trial, and it has felt like that to me this week. Particularly because I've been so busy and exhausted with hospital trips and processing information that I haven't spent any time reading the Bible or being still with God. But in the past few months He has been speaking to me, and in particular Psalm 91 has really impacted me. This is the hope I cling to when I feel hopeless; this brings peace when I feel I am overwhelmed and can't cope. I hope it brings you peace and hope too.

I would also like to add, church is so good for the soul, especially during hardship. It encourages and builds up

and draws you closer to God. I thank God for the church
He's put us in and the way they are helping and
supporting us.

> 'Because he loves me,' says the LORD, 'I will
> rescue him;
> I will protect him, for he acknowledges my
> name.
> He will call on me, and I will answer him;
> I will be with him in trouble,
> I will deliver him and honour him.
> With long life I will satisfy him
> and show him my salvation.'
> (Psalm 91:14-16)

12
In God I Trust

Early June 2016. I was scheduled to have six cycles of chemotherapy that were to be separated by three-week intervals.

This was my first one.

I had to be in hospital all day, as they spaced things out and gave the medication to me slowly so that they could monitor everything and watch for any bad reactions. My day bag was packed with pre-loaded TV programmes on my tablet; the new worship album my sister had given me the day before was on my old MP3 player. I also took a couple of books and some crossword puzzles – as it turned out, this was far too ambitious, and I was really only in the mood to watch TV and listen to music. At least I knew for next time.

Things didn't get off to a good start. A slight problem with my first cannula caused me to have a fainting spell. I then had to wait for half an hour with my legs up and a fan blowing on me before trying again.

The second cannula went in OK, but then as soon as the saline came through I fainted once more. After that they gave me some medication to calm me down. It was strange

– in my head I was calm and fine with everything, but obviously my body had other ideas. It was in no mood to listen to my brain, no matter how many times I tried to calm down. In the end, I just ended up praying and that seemed to work.

It was at this point that one of the other patients encountered a problem and started screaming. She was experiencing back pain – a side effect of one of her medications. Various nurses and doctors came in and soon had her sorted. But this did not do too much to help calm me down, that's for sure.

At the start of the process, they gave me all sorts of medicines to prepare my body for the chemotherapy. These were pre-emptive things to counteract possible side effects. Then a few hours later it began.

There are various types of chemo. I had what is called R-CHOP, a combination of medicines designed to target and kill fast-multiplying cells. The hope was that this would shrink the tumours and bring them under control. I would be having no operations to cut out the lumps. That would be rather difficult as they were all in the lymphatic system that runs throughout the body, which is a vital part of the immune system. It was also suggested that by cutting out this type of cancer, dangerous cells could be released into the rest of the body. But left as it was it could be contained within the lymphatic system.

I discovered that the chemotherapy medicines are light sensitive. This meant when they were hung up on the drip pole, they had to be covered by dark plastic bags, which made it look rather strange. I also had to have some of the chemotherapy medication 'pushed' into the cannula at various intervals by syringe. One of these medications was bright red, and made my urine turn bright red for a while, which was quite amusing.

The rest of my treatment that day went without incident. It lasted seven and a half hours in total.

After the treatment was over, I was sent home with two large carrier bags filled with medications to take in the coming three weeks. They were mostly pills but they had also given me another supply of those self-injecting syringes. It was a job to work out a system to help manage all of them, the times of day they need to be taken, along with whether they need to be taken before or after food.

The nurses and volunteers in the Macmillan unit[21] at the Queen Elizabeth Hospital were so friendly and kind. It really was a pleasure going there. I felt that I was in safe hands and that everyone had my best interests at heart. Frequent rounds of tea, coffee and biscuits were delivered to my chair and there was also a choice of sandwiches at lunchtime.

Going home was a struggle. My body apparently did not cope well with moving vehicles after chemo. In the car on the way back I felt nauseous and in the end I couldn't hold it in any longer. Thankfully, my mother had come prepared with a sick bag so things didn't get too messy. When we got home I was then able to take some antisickness pills that helped get the nausea under control.

A couple of days after my chemo treatment, my two-year-old daughter woke up with a streaming nose quite unexpectedly, but we had come to learn this was normal for infants. However, if you didn't look at her nose you

[21] Macmillan Brook Unit.

114

wouldn't have noticed any difference in her at all. She was her normal, cheeky self – playing in the sunshine and paddling pool, making imaginary cups of tea with her plastic tea set on the lawn.

However, the slime trail from her nasal passages kept coming and so we started to take note. We took her temperature around lunchtime and it was a little elevated, but not too much. Then we took it again after teatime and it had climbed further – she was ill.

The medical professionals had explained to me that one of the biggest threats while having chemotherapy is the risk of infection. Not only does the chemo kill the cancer cells, but it also kills other cells, including the bone marrow, which is responsible for creating new blood and antibodies – my body's main defence armoury. My immune system was virtually going offline during the course of the treatment over the next six months. So great was the risk, I had been issued with a state-of-the art thermometer to take regular temperature readings of myself. I was also given a special 'red card' that I was to present to the Emergency Room if I had to go in, which bumped me straight to the front of the queue and triggered various protocols. I had a twenty-four-hour hotline number to the hospital and the cancer ward in case I thought I was infected; if my temperature went above 37.5°C I had to phone; if it got to 38°C I needed to go straight to A&E. Even a normal infection that one could usually shake off was potentially life-threatening.

A snotty nose was serious.

My wife and I had given some thought to this potential 'what if' scenario and so we swung into prevention mode.

Basically, this meant that either my wife and daughter would leave home for the duration of the illness, or I would. We both had sets of parents living nearby which made this possible, which was a huge blessing. This time, my wife and daughter packed a bag and headed off to Verity's parents' house.

Meanwhile, I stayed at home and sanitised everything, and after putting any possibly contaminated toys away, I washed my hands and alcohol-gelled them. Something I repeated on a regular basis from then onwards.

On 6th June 2016 I blogged:

> It has been rather quiet in the house tonight. No children's programmes on telly, although I did get to watch a few episodes of a new more grown-up police show. But it's rather lonely without my family around. The bed feels emptier too.
>
> Temperature monitoring of myself has been good so far tonight. I am still in a position where my treatment is not very advanced yet, so my immune system should still be functioning somewhat. I have been told that there will be a window of time within the cycle where I will be particularly vulnerable to infection. But today is only Day Five, so God willing I should be alright. My wife phoned half an hour ago and said that our daughter is indeed ill and they had to give her paracetamol syrup to help her sleep and to bring down her temperature tonight. So I guess we have done the right thing and I do hope she will get better soon so that I can be with them again.

It's funny, when I imagined living a life with cancer or going through the turmoil of chemotherapy, this was not something that entered my mind as something I would have to deal with. It is a steep learning curve! Nevertheless, God is in control. I am safe in His arms. All I can do is trust and wait.

It seemed that snotty noses were indeed infectious and I was not to escape this time.

And so began a day of feeling really bad. I was generally lethargic and did nothing all day except sit in front of the television.

My temperature spiked to 38°C around 6pm, so as instructed I phoned ahead and went straight into hospital. They had already arranged a bed for me so that I could bypass A&E.

Mum and Dad kindly took me in to the hospital.

As I had been admitted, Verity and the children were able to return home.

The staff there were very good. I had my chest X-rayed, and swabs, antibiotics and antiviral drips in order to try to sort out whatever infection I had.

Over the next day, my temperature stabilised, although my feet and buttocks began to become inflamed and started itching like mad. We soon discovered that this was a side effect to one of my prescribed medicines as part of the chemotherapy cocktail – one of the many boxes of pills I had taken home with me to take in between treatments.

I found myself awake in the small hours of the night desperately searching for something to distract me from my terribly itchy feet. Wow, they were itchy. It was like they were hot with itchiness, but the more I scratched the worse it got.

The nurse gave me some antihistamines to try to help, although at that point I thought nothing would.

Three days later, I was well enough to return home.

A few days after that, it was the middle of the night and I woke up in agony. My bones felt like they were on fire. A dull ache crescendoed into a wave of burning pain that crashed over me and coursed through my entire body. I don't think I had ever experienced pain like that before; I could not move.

I summoned what energy I had to wake Verity up, and asked her to fetch me some paracetamol to help dull the pain. After some time, it had done its job enough to take the edge off and I was able to return to some semblance of sleep.

Because I had been admitted into hospital just some days before, owing to the infection, the doctor had decided I needed some extra medication. It was a course of three self-administering injections, in addition to my other daily injections that needed to be into the stomach. These GCSF[22] injections were to stimulate my bone marrow to start producing white blood cells again. I had administered the third dose that evening before bed.

One side effect of this medication is pain in the bones, especially in the hips, lower back and thighs.

I survived the following day on painkillers. The course of injections had finished so the pain subsided, and I was OK for the rest of the week. However, there was some bad news – I would have to have these injections after every

---

[22] Granulocyte colony-stimulating factor.

course of chemo from then onwards until the end of my treatment, and instead of only having three, which they had given me in the first instance, I would now have to take five. During a normal cycle, I was to start taking these bone marrow injections on Day Five as this is when my immunity would be at its lowest.

With all the medications and pill-popping I had to do, I had various alarms set up on my tablet. These would ring all through the day and night, reminding me to take one or other pill. Each time it rang, I took a pill. I felt like I was becoming one of Pavlov's dogs.[23] But if I didn't have the alarm, there was no way I would remember to take them.

At this time, I was also having bouts of nausea. This, coupled with my wife being in the first trimester of pregnancy, often saw both of us lying on the sofa feeling sick together. How romantic.

During this troublesome time, one topic had been on my mind – trust.

While thinking about it I came across various passages in the Bible that fuelled my thoughts. I blogged:

> 17th June 2016
> With so much instability in the world – what do you trust in? Can you trust in anything at all?
> We have the instability of politics – just look at the EU Referendum.
> We have the uncertainty of health – I got cancer very unexpectedly; I thought I was quite a healthy guy!

---

[23] Dogs that were conditioned so that they responded in a certain way whenever a bell rang.

We also find it difficult to trust due to pain and suffering; especially when trust has been broken, we find it more challenging to trust again. However, if our relationships are to succeed, we need to find a way to make the decision to trust again for restoration and forgiveness to be released and our relationships to heal and grow. The thing is, we live in a broken and fallen world. Things are not the way they were supposed to be. People are not who they were created to be – full of sin, pride, envy, etc. If we put our trust in a person or in a thing (such as a political system, a financial institution, etc), we will be let down. Things will get shaken, and unexpected things like a sudden diagnosis of cancer will happen. The question changes to: How will we respond?

When things start to shake and fall, when trouble comes knocking on our door, where do we turn? Who do we trust? Do we close our eyes and hold on tight to the edges of the roller coaster we suddenly find ourselves on and hope for the best? Or do we have a confidence and an inner peace that things will be alright because we know someone who is greater than us and greater than the problem who is in control and has our best interests at heart?

If our trust is placed in something or someone who is apart from this world – in God – He is removed from the broken reality of mistakes and hardship. Yes, He feels our suffering and understands our hurting. But He is removed from the brokenness and sin of this world. He is not broken. He is not going to let us down: 'It is better to take refuge in the LORD than to trust in humans' (Psalm 118:8).

I know God won't let me down because I know God. I know Him well enough that I can trust Him completely. I know Him well enough to know that I can put my life in His hands and I am safe there – no matter what happens.

Trust in the LORD with all your heart
and lean not on your own understanding;
in all your ways submit to him,
and he will make your paths straight.
(Proverbs 3:5-6)

In God I trust!

13
Metaphorical Mountain Climbing

It was the day after my thirty-seventh birthday, and I was back in hospital for my second cycle of chemotherapy.

They call each session a 'cycle' and then you count the days – Day One being the day you go in to have all the drips and injections. Then Day Two is the day after you have had your chemo and so on.

Despite having had another rather sleepless night, this session of chemo went much better than the first – and more quickly too.

Two days before my chemo treatment I went in for a clinic where they took bloods, weighed and measured me. I also had a chat with the consultant who was to decide if I was fit enough to undergo the next cycle of chemo or not. He explained that in two weeks' time I was to have another CT scan where they expected to see at least a 50 per cent reduction to the mass in my abdomen that was giving them grave concerns. If it had reduced enough and I was responding to the current course of treatments, I would continue with them and complete my six cycles in total. If not, they would reassess and either accelerate my treatment or change the treatment plan altogether. I was hoping that the original plan was the one we would continue to use.

My second cycle went much better than the first. Apart from a strange taste in my mouth at one point, which the nurse assured me was quite normal (she even got me a glass of fresh orange juice, bless her), everything went swimmingly. They added in an extra drip of antisickness at the end of all the drips and injections to help prevent another vomiting episode in the car on the way home, and it worked. I now had fifty sick bags dotted about the house and car, just in case.

The very next day I was back at the hospital. Yes, Verity pushed me around in a wheelchair as I was weak and could not manage walking too far, but this time we were there for her – not me. It was time for our twelve-week scan.

We were pleased to learn that everything was going well with the pregnancy and that the due date of our new bundle of joy was now predicted to be 6th January.

It was so good to see that tiny little heart beating. We were also treated to a few stretches and a rolling over episode that we watched on the ultrasound screen. The scan picture we printed off was one where the legs were stretched out, like they were lying on a beach somewhere having a relaxing time. We both thought the new baby was going to be a feisty one.

A couple of days after the scan we shaved my head.

About a week previously, my hair had begun to fall out. It happened gradually with a few wisps coming adrift in the shower. As the days passed, however, the skin on my scalp started to feel tingly and quite sensitive in places and hairs in certain areas became hard and brittle. I would wake up with hair covering my pillowcase; hair falling out in clumps into my breakfast cereal was also quite disturbing. After showering and drying my head, the towel would be covered in hair I could not use it to dry the rest of my body! It was very annoying.

I had reached the point where I wanted to shave it off to help make life a bit easier for myself. However, Verity was quite resistant. She didn't want the baldness to be a constant reminder to her of the disease and all its awful implications. She didn't want to stop seeing *me* and just see the *disease* instead.

We reached a compromise where we cut it really short with some electric clippers.

This only lasted about a day, as still having some hair present meant that it was still falling out everywhere.

The decision was made to shave it off completely.

I took the plunge, and together as a family we shaved my head.

It was a lot colder than I imagined. My brain quite often translated 'cold scalp' as me having 'wet hair' so I was constantly checking that I hadn't wet the back of the sofa or my hat.

After a few days, Verity had got used to it and it didn't remind her of the disease as much as she had feared it might.

Katrina took to stroking my bald head and she would give it a kiss every night before bed.

Those who knew me well were aware that I was quite a hairy man, and at that time I could report that hair in all other locations appeared to remain intact for the time being. My consultant told me, however, that by the end of my third cycle I would be completely bald – and he meant all the hair on my entire body. Indeed, I did lose all my body hair eventually, but it took a little longer than he suggested it would.

Even in the event of losing my hair, I knew God was in control. In a passage in the Bible where Jesus teaches us not to worry, He says that God is so intimately involved in each of our lives that He even knows the number of hairs on our head. And even the lack of hairs, in my case.

> Don't be afraid of those who want to kill your body; they cannot touch your soul. Fear only God, who can destroy both soul and body in hell. What is the price of two sparrows – one copper coin? But not a single sparrow can fall to the ground without your Father knowing it. And the very hairs on your head are all numbered. So don't be afraid; you are more valuable to God than a whole flock of sparrows.
> (Matthew 10:28-31, NLT)

He desires to care for us, but will not force the issue. We need to ask for His help. And goodness – I was asking!

Later that month I noticed some other side effects that developed around that time. There was a more persistent nausea (although no vomiting) as well as a strange, stuffy smell in the house that seemed to aggravate it. I believe the strange smell was another side effect of the treatment as no one else could smell it.

I also noticed that shortly after the chemo blast I struggled to find words – especially when I was a bit weary or not feeling too great. I couldn't think of certain words to complete sentences, or I had to describe something to someone else for them to help me find the word I was looking for. This would last for about a week and then I would improve through the cycle.

I had a metallic taste on the roof of my mouth that came and went. I think it had something to do with the steroids I had to continue taking for five days after the chemo – but maybe not.

My tastes were also affected as my stomach would turn at the thought of eating anything too sweet.

These side effects did not make me feel sad or angry. They were simply an accepted part of the treatment, unpleasant as they were.

In early July 2016, I went back into school for the first time since all this had begun. It was an incredibly happy day. My heart was full. I was invited as the guest of honour at the school's fun run that was raising funds for a cancer charity. It was good to see everyone again. My name was emblazoned on the backs of so many of the runners. I had the honour of cutting the starting ribbon to begin the run.

Despite the cold wind, mud and rain, spirits were high and everyone bravely completed the 5km course one way or the other. The hamburgers and hot dogs at the end were great too.

I was so grateful for everyone who ran 'for me', and with more than 250 people taking part I knew a lot of money was raised for an incredibly good cause.

A couple of days later, I was back at the hospital for my second CT scan, the results of which would be discussed at my next clinic with the consultant.

Also, the time had come for us to bid farewell to our house.

Verity had done a great job over the past few weeks packing up our entire house into cardboard boxes. I helped where I could, but the chemo had wiped me out, so I was not doing very much. She had done well and managed to cope without much assistance from me.

Amid the heavy rain, the mountain of cardboard boxes in the house was removed piece by piece and loaded into a hired van along with all our large items of furniture. Our damp possessions were then loaded into a storage locker for the next two months as we waited for the purchase of our new house to be completed.

I felt quite useless during the move, which upset me a little. Usually I would be carrying, pushing and shoving boxes and beds about. But I just couldn't. I had no strength and no stamina. All I did was sit on the sofa at my parents-in-law's house and feel sorry for myself.

In this interim period of being without a house to live in, my family moved into my in-laws' home. It was to be where we would live for the next two months.

A week or so after the move, I was back in hospital again to find out the results of the CT scan. The good news was that the tumours had reduced in size. The bad news was that they had not reduced enough. The doctors were not willing to say that there had been a 'good' response.

This meant there were some discussions about the possibility of my chemotherapy cocktail changing from R-CHOP to R-Bendamustine, a more aggressive treatment. However, the consultants had a meeting with the experts at Addenbrooke's Hospital and 3D measuring was done of my scan. It turned out that the reduction in tumour size was right on the cusp of being 50 per cent, so they were then happy for me to remain on the R-CHOP treatment. This was great news. I felt very relieved, as I was anxious not to be put on the more aggressive treatment plan.

When the doctor told us the not-so-positive result, which turned out to be positive, Verity smiled. This was not the reaction he was expecting and he gave her a bit of a funny look back. The thing was, we both knew that God was up to something. This journey was not an easy one. In fact, if we had come across an easy section I am sure we would have both been rather suspicious. It came as no surprise that there was yet another twist in the tale.

On 13th July 2016 I blogged:

> If you have ever been mountain-climbing before, the experience is similar. You are tired, your muscles are aching. All you want to do is get to the top. Mainly so you can have a rest, but also because it will mean you have achieved your objective – you have endured and overcome the obstacles and have reached the end. Looking up, you see what you think is the summit. You convince yourself that in just a little while you will have made it to the top. But as you approach

it, more of the mountain rises behind it. It is not the summit at all. There is still a long way to go. I am convinced that I will reach the top of this particular mountain. I do not believe I am going to die – yet. God has still got too much for me to do. I have got too much life left to live. But I've still got a mountain to climb – and I've not reached the summit yet. The good thing is I am not climbing alone. I am supported by a great network of friends and family around the world who are praying for me and supporting me. And when the storm clouds roll in and the visibility on the mountainside fades to nothing; when the climb gets tough and when my body just wants to give up, this is when I become more aware of my climbing companion. He is always there – showing me which way to turn; providing comfort to salve my injuries. I am securely tied to Him who is on the other end of my safety rope; He is one step ahead, further up, hammering in the pins to the rock face to keep me secure. I am not alone. Jesus is with me!

14
Leadership and Legacy

It was mid-July and I was now at the half way point of my scheduled cycles of chemotherapy.

> 15th July 2016
> It continues to surprise me that I actually have cancer. It is quite a difficult thing to get my head around, especially when each time I go into hospital I go in feeling fine and, after having treatment, leave feeling bad. For some days after the treatment, especially this time, I often find myself looking at the puncture mark on the top of my hand where the cannula was during the chemo, my hand yellowing a little with bruising, thinking about how such toxic chemicals are being pumped into my body to do me good. It is hard to reconcile the idea in my brain.

The next few days saw ups and downs in terms of having waves of nausea. My energy levels were also fluctuating. I was not up to doing very much. This meant that I missed going to the zoo with the family to celebrate my wife's birthday, missed taking my two-year-old daughter to the swimming pool and missed going to church on Sunday. I felt useless and was sad that I was missing out on spending time with my family. Although, as my mother reminded me, I was not 'doing nothing', I was giving my body the time it needed to recover and to heal.

On the other hand, I needed to keep reminding myself that it was for those very reasons that I was undergoing the treatment – so that I could take part in many more birthday celebrations and trips to the swimming pool with my wife and children in the months and years to come. It was a matter of perspective.

I filled my days watching back-to-back episodes of TV series box sets. All that was required was enough energy to lie on the sofa and occasionally press a button on the remote control – I could cope with that.

18th July 2016

I must admit that during the past few months I have not spent much alone time with God. It was great that I was able to have that time away just before my diagnosis to help me process and pray. But since then, I seem to have been caught up in a whirlwind of treatments and hospital visits, not to mention the sale of our house coming through and the packing of the house and moving out, etc, etc. Then there are days when I just don't feel 'up to it'. Now I'm thinking that I am making excuses, but I think God is OK with it. He knows me and He knows what is going on in my life right now. I'm not perfect by any means.

I did manage to do a little bit of songwriting yesterday evening. I was amazed that I was inspired (as this is not an everyday occurrence). Neither of the songs is finished – I have got two possible choruses… I think. But it was fun, and it was good to realise that I can still do things like that. My voice was scratchy and kept dipping in and out. Maybe it was the time of day, or maybe it was because of the chemo. I'm not sure, but I trust that as time goes on my voice will also heal. I'm not looking forward to this evening. This is Day Five of my treatment cycle, which means that this evening I need to start to give myself the extra GCSF injection in addition to the daily one. Apart from it being very unpleasant having to inject myself in the stomach, doing it twice in quick succession is doubly skin-crawling. Not only that, but these bone marrow injections have the potential to hurt! By about the third or fourth day of these extra injections my bones really start to ache and I have to pile on the painkillers. Sometimes knowing what is to come is not recommended.

Like clockwork, it happened again. After the third injection of the bone marrow stimulant, the much-feared and expected excruciating bone pain caused by the additional injections kicked in.

As in the past, it started slowly in my lower back and spread. There was a continual dull ache punctuated with moments of sharp pain that made me groan or cry out. I was swallowing painkillers throughout the day.

Thankfully, the pain only lasted for about twenty-four hours.

Other side effects I suffered affected all three states of matter[24] in one way or another.

One side effect of the chemotherapy was that I got clogged up. My solids became very solid and could cause problems. The doctors anticipated this so had prescribed constipation medication. Unfortunately, this medicine ran out, which left me with a fissure and blood in my stool, as well as an uncomfortable feeling in my digestive system.

My planned treatment process did not include an operation to surgically remove the tumours. Instead, the idea was to shrink and reduce them purely through chemical means via the medication. This meant that all the toxic chemicals, and all the toxins that were created when the tumours were broken down, left the body in the urine.

To flush this out required me to drink – litres and litres a day. Sometimes I thought it would be easier to permanently attach a tap to my mouth. Drinking so much lead to a lot of toilet time – almost every half an hour! But it needed to be done and in doing so I would avoid the excess toxins causing extra pain upon leaving my body.

It was a leap year, which meant it was also the year of worldwide athletic competition. As the Olympics, held in Rio, drew closer, with the opening ceremony about to happen in early August, the UK press focused quite a lot on the legacy of London, which had hosted the Olympics in 2012. Indeed, a big part of the bid for the 2012 Games was based upon the legacy they would leave behind after they had ended. Different TV programmes were aired

---

[24] A euphemism for liquids, solids and gases – bodily functions!

exploring what effect the 2012 competition had had in encouraging people in the UK to engage more with sport – which showed varying levels of success.

As a result, I was thinking about the legacy we leave as leaders.

Since my cancer treatment had begun, I had pretty much withdrawn from all the leadership roles in my local church ministry that I held, as well as being signed off work for at least six months.

It had been a sudden withdrawal and there had been no time to plan or put extra things in place. People in the ministry had to move quickly from a position of knowing I was not well, and this might mean more of a burden on them in the distant future, to more practical matters, such as who was going to lead the band practice in two days' time.

The people who stepped into the gap for me did an amazing job and I remain so thankful for them to this day. Things didn't grind to a halt. Things didn't collapse. They did fine without me – and this was a good thing.

On 28th July 2016 I blogged:

> How well will our churches or organisations cope without us? What if we got a call from the doctors saying, 'Get here now! We need to operate!' and this meant we were unable to function in our role for several months? Would our churches be able to carry on without us? Have we led and trained up key people in key positions? Are we able to delegate now – even though we are not signed off work?

Sometimes leaders feel that the only way to do something right is to do it themselves – someone else will just mess it up! Letting go and delegating can be difficult, but it is necessary to make us more productive and more effective as leaders.

Are the leaders in our churches able to train and raise up other leaders? If we are leaving a legacy, this is good – if those who follow us are also leaving a legacy, this is excellent.

Leaders should not only focus on the here and now but also on the future. This includes a future without them. Good leaders lead in the here and now. Excellent leaders lead with the future in mind.

It might be time to start thinking about our leadership legacy. I know I am.

15
Bad Blood

It was early August. I had just completed my fourth chemotherapy session. It was by far the worst one yet. Although everything went according to plan and there were no complications or adverse effects, I was not in a good place mentally.

In the days leading up to the chemo I now knew what to expect. How the drugs affected my body, drained my energy, the nausea and the nosedive my quality of life took each cycle. I also hated all the needles! Every time I went to the hospital or visited the doctor I seemed to be greeted with a jab in my arm – a blood test, a cannula, the boxes of injections they stocked me up with to self-administer daily at home.

I was not in my usual positive place. In fact, even thinking about the treatment for months after it was over would make my stomach churn.

It is amazing how powerful the mind is. Owing to my 'down' mental state, my experience of this treatment cycle was adversely affected. I came away feeling slightly more positive but not terribly so. I made it home and ate well. But in the night, the waves of nausea overcame me and had me on my knees in the bathroom vomiting into the toilet at midnight and then again at 5am.

It made sense – my body was trying to purge itself of the poisons that had entered it. Chemo seemed to be such a counterintuitive treatment. Put something into the body to kill certain cells that will ultimately cure you.

Up until this point I did not really understand those who gave up on their treatment before it was over. Surely people knew that in the end it was the right thing to do? But now, I understood. The emotional and mental toll the treatment took was bigger than I had anticipated.

At this point, I was trying to turn my mind around to face another two cycles of treatment. I was determined to go through with them, but it was not going to be an easy descent. Sometimes coming down the mountain was more difficult than the climb up.

A few days after this low emotional point, something positive came along to occupy my mind. Our mortgage application had finally come through and had been approved. So we entered into another time of waiting while the lawyers got everything in order to enable the exchange of contracts to take place. This would get the keys to our new home into our hands.

Later that month I found myself at another consultant appointment.

I learned that apart from general and expected side effects, I was doing well. However, my white blood cell count was down. I admitted to the doctor that of the five of the bone marrow GCSF injections I had been given for this cycle of treatment, I had only managed to have four owing to the intense pain they gave me. So the doctor insisted that in the two days between the appointment and my scheduled treatment, I was to take an additional two injections. This was only to happen this once so that the treatment would be able to go ahead.

However, because I had just had a low count, my consultant wanted me to ensure I took all five of the regularly prescribed GCSF injections during my next cycle.

The good news was that, because of the pain, I would be allowed to split them into two batches – three injections one week, then a break of a few days and then the final two injections the following week. It was hoped that this would alleviate the build-up in my system that caused me the pain.

On 25th August 2016 I wrote:

My eyebrows and eyelashes are getting rather patchy these days. And hair loss is being experienced in other unmentionable regions of my anatomy. I also have spells of pins and needles and numbness in various limbs, more so at night but it can also happen during the day.

As Thursday approaches I am trying to keep my mind on other things – we found out we are having a baby girl at Verity's scan last week, and we got the keys to our new house today! So hopefully this cycle will be less plagued by negativity.

I have been booked in for another scan in late September, as by this time I will have completed my sixth and final cycle of chemo and the doctors want to check that all the tumours have gone, so prayers in the lead-up to this would be most appreciated. I am hoping that things can start to get back to normal if I get the all clear.

The day of my fifth chemotherapy session had arrived. It began with a tricky cannula insertion into the top of my left hand. I always hated this bit. This time I was justified in my dread as it took them a while to find the vein. This sent my body into shutdown mode and I had another fainting episode, complete with moans and groans and nurses rushing around lifting my legs up. Incidentally, this was the same hand cannulated when I had my previous fainting episode during chemotherapy one.

After giving me a while to recover, the medication began. Near the beginning of the treatment, they gave me antihistamines to prevent allergic reactions. They always say that they can make you drowsy. Up until now I had not been too bothered by that, but this time I'm not sure if it was the antihistamines or the fainting, but I felt rotten so I slept through pretty much the entire treatment.

The fifth session of chemotherapy was now over and done. It made me feel just as sick and lacking in energy and pumped as full of toxins as the others had. But my mental attitude was better in the lead-up to it and continued to remain positive afterwards.

This left me with just one more to go! After my sixth cycle, which was planned for September, I had another scan booked so the doctors could assess how the treatment had gone and if my intensive chemotherapy treatment could end for the time being.

On 29th August 2016 I blogged:

My bone injections start again tonight. I am allowed to have three this week, then have a break until the start of next week when I have to take the other two to complete the course. This break should hopefully help alleviate the pain of the bone ache. The doctor has also prescribed me extra pain medication to help me cope.

We move into our new house today! I am ensconced on the sofa at my in-laws' house while family and friends are all rallying round doing the heavy lifting and moving. I do feel bad because I want to be doing it; I am just physically unable. I can't wait to get back to normal.

Although I have not been doing too much praying and Bible-reading during this time, I have felt God close to me. He has prompted me to read a book in the Bible about a guy called Job who had an even rougher deal than I am currently experiencing. I am finding it interesting seeing the similarities and differences in my situation as compared to his and am drawing hope and strength from it.

16
I Want to Grow Old

It was the start of September and things in the current cycle had been going fairly well until now. Things down below had started to sting more than usual when I went to the toilet. A common side effect that I had suffered from continually during my treatment was chronic constipation. At the time I thought nothing of it – it was something that was commonplace, and I just had to put up with it. However, it was quite a hot day and by the evening I was curled up on the sofa under a blanket, shivering.

We took my temperature, and it was 37.7°C. This was over the threshold of 37.5°C so I had to call the special chemotherapy helpline number. They advised me to come into the hospital straight away as they were going to admit me. I had an infection.

I really did not want to go in as now my mind had associated hospital with chemo sessions that made me feel terrible. I had to overcome a mental battle to pack my bags and go.

In hospital, my blood tests revealed that I had virtually no white blood cells. This meant I was classed as neutropenic and was rushed into an isolation room. I was hooked up to a variety of intravenous drips throughout my stay – it was quite hard to keep up with it all.

While I was in isolation, Verity and Katrina came to see me. Technically, I wasn't allowed to have children visit. But I put my foot down and insisted that I was allowed to see my own daughter. We had to have our visit in a special side room and not on the ward or in my isolation room. Katrina had started to get used to visiting me in hospital. She enjoyed sitting on the hospital bed with me and pressing all the buttons to make the bed move, although she didn't like the needles and the plasters. This visit, being in a different room with no beds, made it rather a strange one for her.

After a couple of days, a space opened up on the specialist cancer ward. I loved it there as the staff's specialist knowledge made me feel safe, and I had also got to know the nurses and doctors as I had been in a few times now.

As each day went by, I began to respond to the medication and started to improve. They gave me extra bone marrow injections, which caused the aching as usual, but they did the trick and my neutrophil[25] levels increased.

I was also on laxatives to help with my bowel movements. At least things were moving. The pain down under became not so constant and only occurred when on the toilet. By this stage, the rest of me was feeling OK and blood tests showed I was no longer infected. So I was discharged.

On 3rd September 2016 I blogged:

---

[25] A kind of white blood cell.

The other day I watched a silly movie with my wife. It was not my usual type of movie, a bit rude in places, but only rated 12, so no need to panic. It explored the relationships of lifelong friends who were now octogenarians, so as you can imagine there was a fair amount of reminiscing about the good old days.

The thing that struck me was that – I want to grow old!

This may sound like a revolutionary statement. We are constantly being told we need to stay young. Buy the latest serum to keep your skin looking youthful and do everything you can to cover up those grey hairs!

But I have come to realise, being diagnosed with cancer, that this is all a load of rubbish. I want to grow old. I never even contemplated that this would be a desire in my life. Somehow it was inevitable. I was always going to grow old. I was always going to be around for as long as the world would have me. Surely everyone gets old? Well, maybe not.

There is much to be said about living for the future, for setting goals and pursuing dreams. I still have dreams that I am pursuing. But I am also looking more closely at the here and now. Right here in the everyday and the mundane. In the grit of living real life – right here, today – right now. It is often a cliché to say, 'Live every day as if it were your last,' but what if it was? Would I do anything differently? Would I focus more or less of my energy and time on a particular thing or person? What really matters?

I want to grow old. I realise this stage of life terrifies many people, which is why we work so hard to put it off for as long as possible. Yes, it may come with added hardships, with extra aches and pains, with bodies that no longer function like they used to. We might forget things more easily or get a disease like Alzheimer's. It may also signify being fewer steps away than we would like to eternity – but I have come to realise, we are as close to death right now as we ever will be. We never know when our time may come.

The Bible speaks of old age in quite a different way than we view it in society today. Those in old age are to be honoured and respected. They are to be listened to as they have wisdom that we can all benefit from. 'Grey hair is a crown of splendour; it is attained in the way of righteousness' (Proverbs 16:31). 'Wisdom is with the aged, and understanding in length of days' (Job 12:12, ESV).

So yes – I want to grow old!

My wife will tell you that I haven't been one to make much of celebrating my birthday. It all stems from my secondary boarding school education where some unkind people would make your life unpleasant if they discovered that it was your birthday. You learned to keep your mouth shut and your head down and treat the day as you would any other to avoid any unpleasantness. However, this experience has shown me that this attitude needs to change.

Life is precious.

Life is a gift.

Life is certainly worth celebrating!

So I will mark each day with a prayer of thanks for the opportunity and privilege of living it and I will celebrate life whenever I have the opportunity, even if it means eating cake.

I was now at home. However, down under still hurt pretty badly. The doctor found a tear and a haemorrhoid, so going to the toilet was very painful.

I had an appointment at the hospital coming up in a few days' time where they would assess whether I was able to undergo my final chemo session or not.

I felt I was so close to the finish line, but yet so far. There were still many mountains to climb before I was through. It was becoming exhausting, and I was getting fed up with it.

However, I was determined to have my final session of chemo, whenever it was. But I really, really, really didn't want to go through with it. Just the thought of it made my stomach turn. Wow – chemo made me feel *so* sick! I hated it. Yet it was my only option if I was to choose life. Therefore, I gritted my teeth and got on with it.

People have called me brave, but I wasn't, really. Jesus made me brave. Without Him there was no way I would have been able to cope – no way at all. It was amazing how much courage Jesus gave me.

Thankfully, my sixth chemotherapy session did happen as planned and it went well. I am pleased to say there was nothing much to report. There were no unexpected happenings or nasty surprises. Everything went as it should and even a bit quicker than I was used to.

I was glad I had decided to take in my own supply of food for lunch as my brain now associated hospital sandwiches and hospital coffee with the awful nauseous feeling chemo gave me. I had also gone off crisps (even the ones at home) for the same reason.

I was booked in for a PET[26] CT scan, for a 3D image, at Norfolk & Norwich University Hospital in a month's time. This would give the doctors a good picture of what had gone on and where we now stood.

It was going to be quite an arduous scan. I was not allowed to eat anything for six hours before. I would be injected with a radioactive isotope, then wait an hour (no reading or writing, but I could listen to music). I would then have to lie still for half an hour in a big machine. The worst part was because I would be radioactive for a while I had to avoid contact with pregnant mothers or young children, so I would have to spend the rest of the day away from Katrina and Verity. We had arranged for me to sleep at my parents' house that night.

My appointment with the consultant was booked for the first week of November where we would be discussing the way forward. We were at a strange stage in the process. The six chemo sessions had finished so we were now in a period of limbo, not knowing what the next steps would be until the scan and appointment had happened.

Would I need further treatment? Would I be able to return to work? No one knew. One thing we were certain of was that at some point, I would need to go into the day

---

[26] Positron emission tomography.

surgery unit to have my kidney stent removed, but as for the timing of this – you've guessed it – no one knew.

17
Faith in the Fog

I had just had my final chemotherapy session, and so I had to start my last lot of GCSF injections. This time the doctor had prescribed some extra pain medication to help alleviate my suffering.

I was a little busy over the weekend, as I attended a church conference in a nearby village and then also went to church on Sunday. This did take its toll, so for the following week I was determined to take it easy as I did not want to end up in hospital again.

On 25th September 2016 I wrote:

> Wow – Friday was a day of pain!
> I took my fourth GCSF injection on Thursday evening. Based on past experience, the fourth injection causes the pain. This one did not disappoint. Friday was a day of pain. In fact, I think it was the most painful it has ever been. I was totally incapacitated on the sofa, popping painkillers like sweets. At one point in the afternoon, even the sofa was too painful to sit on, so I went and lay in bed for a few hours – if I didn't move the pain subsided a little.

The bone ache was centred on my chest and lower back. The chest pain made it difficult to breathe at times. When it gets really bad, the pain comes in waves along with your pulse – these were the times that made me moan and groan the most. Poor Verity, she hates hearing the painful moaning.

The pain was so bad and so debilitating that I refused to take the fifth injection on Friday night. Enough was enough! A sign that the injections are working is the bone ache. I had ached enough, so I am sure the bone marrow has been stimulated enough. I have been keeping a close eye on my temperature and that is stable, so no signs of infection.

This meant that I was in a reasonable enough state to go with Verity and Katrina to the fair on Saturday afternoon and enjoy watching her go on the 'spinny spinny' as she calls the rides. That to me is much more like living life than lying in a bed and moaning.

It was early October. All through the ordeal we had been keeping our church family up to date with the ups and downs of our ordeal. We thought it would be fitting to invite family and friends to our new home that we had just moved into for a time of prayer and thanksgiving. This had been organised by my wife. Those from the local area squeezed into our lounge and those from further afield, notified by Facebook, joined in with prayers from afar.

There was a prolonged time of prayer for my healing from cancer, as well as thanks for getting me this far.

At the time we were in a fog as far as answering the question, 'Where do we go from here?' My planned course of chemotherapy had come to an end. I was due for the PET CT scan on Monday and then I had to wait for the results, which I would get on 1st November. We were very much in a holding pattern as we waited for tests, scans and then decisions as to what the next steps would be.

We also prayed about the next steps, asking Jesus to heal me completely (as this was something medical science cannot do for my type of cancer), as well as returning to work and 'normal' life.

The elders of the church anointed me with oil, as the Bible instructs:

> Is anyone among you ill? Let them call the elders
> of the church to pray over them and anoint them
> with oil in the name of the Lord. And the prayer
> offered in faith will make the sick person well;
> the Lord will raise them up.
> (James 5:14-15)

Even in this time of fog, I had faith. I knew that in the middle of uncertainty I could be certain in Christ. He was an unmovable and unchanging rock to which I could cling in times of doubt and darkness (and still can). Without Jesus, I would have been adrift and all at sea, and most probably drowning in the worry and stress of it all.

Messages had been flooding in from friends all over the world saying that they too were praying for me and my family, which were greatly appreciated.

Five days after the prayer gathering, I travelled to Norfolk & Norwich University Hospital for the PET CT scan. I was determined to stick to the strict 'no eating before the scan' policy, as I woke up at 4am to eat some scrambled eggs on toast for breakfast while I was still allowed to do so. I did manage to get back to sleep afterwards, which was good.

The scan was uneventful. As expected, it consisted of lots of sitting around and waiting as well as answering endless questions on endless forms. It was quite a chilly, rainy day. The mobile unit that held the scanner was fairly warm and comfortable, which was good, because after being injected I had to sit and wait for an hour for the radioactive tracer to circulate around my system. I was glad I had brought my old MP3 player so I could listen to music. I was feeling calm and wasn't worried at all.

Once in the scanning room I couldn't help noticing how cold it was, as opposed to the warmth in the rest of the mobile unit. The air conditioning was blowing, and it felt a bit like a fridge. I discovered later that the machine gets quite hot, so this probably explains the need for the chill in the scanning room air. I lay on the bed of the scanner as it whooshed in and out of the doughnut-shaped hole – all the while with my hands above my head. The tunnel was longer than that of a normal CT scanner, which I was not expecting. And in this scan the bed was raised as high as it could go to the top of the doughnut hole without my bent knees touching it.

As the machine whirred and clicked and the bed I was lying on moved backwards and forwards, I almost fell asleep.

After half an hour I was extracted from the doughnut and sent on my way. I was pleased to find the hospital café close by so I could get some food inside my belly.

No results were given on the day. The images were sent to my consultant and I already had an appointment with him to discuss the results in the coming weeks.

On 15th October 2016 I blogged:

> Don't you find that a lot of life consists of a 'hurry up and wait' mentality? You hurry because you are running late and you're going to miss your doctor's appointment. When you get there, just in time, you have to sit and wait. You are desperately trying to get the shopping done before heading home to make lunch on time for the kids. Then you get to the tills and you have to wait.
>
> Life consists of times of action and times of waiting (as well as many others). I have entered a time of waiting. My chemotherapy treatments and multiple trips to the hospital for them, scans and the occasional hospital sleepover have ended. I have had my PET scan and now I am waiting for the results – hurry up and wait.
>
> There are times when I find my mind wandering into dangerous territory. The big 'what if' questions start to emerge. What if it hasn't gone? What if I need more treatment? What if this storm is not over for the moment? What if I can't go back to work? What if… what if… what if…
>
> When I begin to hear the 'what ifs' echoing in my mind I need to remind myself that it's OK. God is in control. He always has been and He always

will be. He is unchanging and I can trust Him. He was firmly in control of my life from the beginning of this journey with cancer. In fact, He has been there even before all that – and He will continue to be.

I was due to have my appointment with my consultant on 25th October. However, we have a big family holiday booked over that week. You know, the sort where masses of extended family get together for a week's holiday; not sure whether it is a good idea or not. We have luckily done it before, so it should be fine. As my wife has cancelled absolutely every outing and family activity throughout this summer due to my ill health, hospital visits, treatments, scans, etc, I am not going to miss this one! Especially as I am now off chemo and am feeling almost back to my normal self. My immunity is almost back to normal and my hair is even starting to grow back. So I have pushed the results appointment back a week to the 1st November.

No matter how long I have to wait and no matter what comes, whatever the outcome of the results, I can trust God. He is holding me. He is in control. I just need to remind myself of this at times.

18
Remission Accomplished

On 1st November 2016 I wrote:

> Today I had an appointment with my consultant where I found out about how well my chemotherapy treatment had gone and what was going on inside my body by finding out the results of the PET scan.
>
> It is good news! The doctors say that my scan revealed no living cancer cells in my body. I still have a small mass of scar tissue of dead cells (approximately 7cm x 3cm) where the massive tumour in my abdomen used to be, but it has drastically reduced in size and they are dead and no longer active. I am now in complete remission. Praise God!
>
> However, I am still 'in treatment'. Now begins a two-year course of treatment to prolong the extent of the remission, as I have been told that at present modern medicine cannot completely kill the type of cancer I have got, so they do expect it to return at some point – although I

believe in a God of miracles so continue to trust in my complete healing.

I now need to go back to the hospital once every two months to have a two-hour drip of Rituximab after having all the usual pre-meds. This formed part of my chemotherapy cocktail, but I don't think it counts as chemo on its own, although they still call it 'chemo' – I guess it's easier. I may still be susceptible to a low white blood cell count but should not feel as ill or as wiped out as I did when having chemotherapy.

My daily self-administered injection into the stomach to thin my blood in order to reduce the risk of blood clots can now stop. Hurray!

My stent is scheduled to be removed on Thursday 10th November in the day surgery unit. I should be in and out within a couple of hours. This is good as recently I have had the odd twinge in the location of my stent, so it is probably time it came out.

My hair is also making a comeback. My head hair is fairly normal. I haven't noticed any 'chemo curl' that a lot of other patients have talked to me about. I now have quite a few more grey hairs (but not as many as my wife was expecting, apparently). I must say it is strange having quite a lot of patches of stubble in various locations all over my body.

My scan also revealed something unexpected. They found a small 'nodule' on one of my lungs. It did not 'light up' in the scan so they do not think it is cancerous but I will be booked in for further scans in the near future so they can monitor it.

As far as returning to work is concerned, I am all set for a phased return in mid-January as the doctors want to see how I respond to my first Rituximab treatment first. However, at present I am allowed to go in for 'Keep in Touch' days so I can keep up to date with INSET[27] and go to a meeting or two just so I can begin to dip my toes back into the waters.

My journey continues but the path is getting easier and wider. I can now see further into the distance. There are places ahead where I can stop, sit and appreciate the view and the company. One thing I can count on is that I know Jesus will continue to be with me every step of the way.

We had been waiting for this day to come since we first heard the word 'cancer' all those months earlier. We had been looking ahead to the day I would be told that the cancer was no longer in my body. This is the day when the trumpets should have been heralding the victory cry, 'It is over.'

Yet it did not feel like this at all. It did not feel like the battle was over and it certainly did not feel like I had won. This was just a step along a very long road. It was the end of the current plan of action, but another plan of action was to follow. There was more to come and the dark cloud

[27] In-service Education and Training. This is a teacher-training day, when children don't come into school.

of cancer could return at any moment where we would have to face this all over again. I still might not grow old.

It was at this moment that God gave Psalm 92 to my wife as an encouragement to us both:

> The righteous will flourish like a palm tree,
> they will grow like a cedar of Lebanon;
> planted in the house of the LORD,
> they will flourish in the courts of our God.
> They will still bear fruit in old age,
> they will stay fresh and green,
> proclaiming, 'The LORD is upright;
> he is my Rock, and there is no wickedness in him.'
> (Psalm 92:12-15)

The adversaries are defeated.

I will flourish.

I will still bear fruit in my old age – I will grow old.

Lord, You have truly made me glad by Your deeds. I will forever praise You.

The day for my stent removal had arrived. I was in the Day Surgery unit and was very pleased not to be in A&E or the cancer ward.

When I went for my pre-operation assessment the week before the procedure, they still had me down on their paperwork as needing a *replacement*. I let them know what the consultant had told me and suggested that the surgeon and my consultant discuss what was to be done before my operation.

It was now the day of the operation and I still had not heard if I was having a removal or a replacement. When I arrived, most of the team in charge of me had got the message from the consultant that I was having my stent removed. However, one of the doctors was insisting I should have a replacement – until I stood my ground, and he went to speak to the surgeon. It turned out that I was indeed right, and a removal was definitely what I was having.

Owing to this confusion, the same chap then said that removals were usually done under local anaesthetic, not general. Although this option was far less appealing to me – as being awake while someone fiddled with my nether regions did not appeal – I accepted it. I kept telling myself that it could be far worse – I could be having chemo.

I walked to the anaesthetic room to be prepared for the operation. It was a slightly uncomfortable experience because as I walked into the room I heard someone say, 'Oh, hello, Mr McChlery. It's good to see you again. You used to teach my children.' This was quite embarrassing owing to the intimate nature of my procedure!

As I was being wheeled into the operating theatre, I had a dizzy sensation – then I blacked out. They had given me a general anaesthetic after all.

The operation did not last long. I was soon awake in the recovery room. Then through to the ward and eating a sandwich and drinking a cup of coffee.

I was home again by early evening.

There was a slight ache where my stent used to be, and going to the toilet stung a little. But all in all, everything was fine, and I was on the mend.

On 12th November 2016, I was one of around 500 delegates who made their way to central London for the tenth annual Premier Digital Awards and Conference. The conference happened during the day, with thirty-six contributors and six 'streams' to choose from to equip and empower the Church to share its faith in the digital space. There were some thought-provoking and challenging keynote addresses.

I attended two sessions in the morning in the 'Creators' stream where I learned more about blogging. It was good to know I was already doing quite a lot of it right – but there were golden nuggets of advice, and practical tips. Then the afternoon saw me in the 'Growing Community' stream where we learned about how digital can help churches build stronger communities as well as reach out to their wider community.

I was back again for the very posh awards dinner in the evening with Verity as I had been awarded 'Finalist' position in the 'Accessibility' category for my church's website and again in the 'Most Inspiring Leadership Blog' for the blog I had been writing about my journey with faith and cancer. Unfortunately, in both categories I did not win, but was very pleased to be recognised by this national award for the work that I did and to know that the contribution I made in the digital space was significant and meaningful.

Three days later, I trod the now all-too familiar path back to the Queen Elizabeth Hospital in King's Lynn. This time I was there for my first maintenance treatment.

This would be the first of twelve cycles that were scheduled to last approximately two years. By having this treatment, the hope was that any possible relapse I may have in the future would get pushed further and further away.

To my delight, it turned out that my maintenance treatment was much shorter than the chemotherapy. It only took three hours as opposed to all day.

I arrived at 12 noon with some bacon sandwiches that I had brought with me, as the hospital ones still made me nauseous.

I had another cannula inserted successfully. No fainting this time. I still had to have pre-meds that consisted of paracetamol and antihistamines to help my body not react badly to the medication.

Half an hour after this, I had the two-hour drip of Rituximab. Having had Rituximab as part of the chemo cocktail, my body was already used to it.

Everything went well. It felt strange leaving empty-handed – no bags full to bursting with medication for me to continue to take at home.

I was also feeling fine. No nausea, just a heavy sense of drowsiness, which was about the only side effect of this maintenance treatment, apart from a slightly lowered immunity – but nothing as bad as when I was having the full chemotherapy.

19
A New Arrival

December 2016. What an unexpected thrill to have a haircut. I'm not being sarcastic – I mean it. There were moments during my chemotherapy when the thoughts of having a haircut again were but distant dreams and fantasies. I walked into the barbers with such joy in my heart – I was having a haircut. It was an everyday, mundane activity that I had the privilege to be experiencing again. The small things served as huge landmarks along the road of recovery. Life was getting back to normal, and I was still around to enjoy it.

My schedule had been filling up too. I ran the end-of-term Christmas disco at school and had organised and taken part in the Wisbech Churches Together[28] 'Walking Nativity' at the Wisbech Christmas Market. However, I learned that building up one's strength and stamina after a major illness takes a lot longer than I thought it would. I would have liked to be operating at full steam again. I was feeling better, after all. But it would take a long time for

---

[28] A network that draws together Christians of all church backgrounds and encourages unity and mutual cooperation.

me to get back to full physical strength, even if mentally I felt fine. There were times I found I had to stop myself to take a break. Or I would catch myself walking way too fast and found I was getting out of breath.

At this stage, Verity's baby bump seemed to be growing daily. It had reached the point where something was always aching. Our little one was a wriggler and could often move into uncomfortable and sometimes painful positions for Verity. My wife's ability to pick up things from the floor or carry anything had become seriously impeded, as it had during her last pregnancy. We technically had about three weeks until the due date, but our little one could arrive at any time.

The nursery had by now been decorated, and awaited its new resident. I was looking forward to being 'Daddy' to a second little girl, and I was so grateful that I was able to be around to be part of her precious life.

Two days after Christmas, a friend of mine died. He too had cancer, and had been diagnosed a few months before I was. During chemotherapy, we messaged each other a few times comparing experiences, as well as the lack of hair. He was also a musician and was a Christian.

When I heard the news about his death, I was not prepared for the range of emotions that came over me.

It suddenly brought everything back – all those feelings of sadness when I was first diagnosed. I kept thinking, 'That could be me. That could be me.' We had had such a happy Christmas, made all the sweeter that I was there to share in it. But my friend's Christmas was very different.

Our lives and journeys were similar and intersected on a variety of levels, yet he was gone and I was still here. I guess I had a bit of survivor's guilt. I just needed to accept that I would never understand God's entire plan for our lives. Even in the middle of sorrow, God was still God and He was still in control. Even though my friend had died of the very thing that could have killed me (and still could), I still chose to trust God. I still clung to my Rock. He who was able to remain steady and stable in the middle of any storm.

On 28th December 2016, I wrote:

> Your gentleness and friendship will not be forgotten. You are now free from the pain and suffering of this world. I'm sure everyone up there with you is dancing along with your trumpet playing – how great that must be! I look forward to joining in when my time comes. A fanfare for a friend.

The long-expected moment had come. Although it was a couple of days after the due date, Verity went into labour at 4am on 8th January 2017. By 8am we were asked to come into hospital and by 9.30am our second child had arrived safe and sound. Welcome to the world, Lara.

A few tears were shed – I was there. I was still alive.

Lara means 'protected one' and encapsulated all our hopes and prayers for her during the pregnancy and, indeed, into her new little life.

Lara was truly a miracle. She had been conceived at the last possible moment before my chemotherapy began, which could have left me infertile. God's timing was perfect. He was in control and I knew I could trust Him –

even if His answer was no. Thankfully, this time it was a yes.

It was now mid-January. It did not seem like it had been two months since my last maintenance treatment, but it was. At the recent clinic, my consultant was pleased with my progress. He also mentioned that from looking at my weight chart he saw that I had had a good Christmas. I had put on weight – and had done so throughout my chemotherapy. For six months before my diagnosis, I had been on a diet and had lost 12kg. But during chemo I felt I had enough on my plate without having to worry about my weight too, so I let it slide. Now that I was healthy again, I really did need to start the diet once more to try to get back to where I had been before the chemo, if only to be able to fit into the new clothes I had just bought before it all happened.

The nurses were excited to see the photos on my phone of Lara, and were so pleased that I was able to be there, and that cancer had not got the better of me.

However, there was trouble with the cannula.

By now, I had a reputation among the chemo nurses of being a fainter when they put the cannula in. We tried my right hand (the one that coped better). The first nurse tried twice with two different cannulas without success. Then a second nurse had a go, but she too was unsuccessful. By this time, they said I was going a funny colour, so out came the fan and all the usual embarrassing procedures occurred.

Another nurse came along and, after a little while, she tried to put it in my left hand. This time it went in. Hurray.

I didn't actually faint, but I ended up with the back of my hands feeling like a pincushion.

The rest of the treatment was fine. I was so glad I had discovered the hospital had free Wi-Fi in the treatment room. It meant I could stream some TV programmes without having to download them first.

As happened last time, the treatment made me feel very drowsy. But that was all. The next day I was up and about and leading a 'Digital Disciples' workshop for my local Wisbech Churches Together.

20
The Illusion of Control

It was now nearing the end of the first month of 2017. I had reached a point in my recovery where I was feeling a bit more able to do some of the things I had been doing before I became ill. One of those milestones along the road of recovery was a trip up to Blackburn to give an after-dinner speech. I shared my testimony about the events of 2016 as chronicled in my blog, and how God had been working in and through my life.

I stayed the night with my brother-in-law and his fiancée who lived in Manchester. Then I made my way back home the following day; a round trip of 400 miles.

The next day, my phased return to work began. It went really well. I was helping with the Year Three class as it was the largest in the school and needed an extra pair of hands.

I mostly listened to the children read their reading books, and signed their reading records as well as writing down their spelling test results.

I was only in school for three hours and didn't do very much in the grand scale of things, but having had a period of about six months where I had literally been doing nothing, I was exhausted.

I was due to go back in to work for three days a week where I would stay for a few hours each time. This proved to be a gentle and necessary time for me to get back into the swing of work, both mentally and physically.

Early March and I was back in hospital as an outpatient for my next two-monthly maintenance treatment. It was amazing how quickly two months came around.

Yet again the nurses had trouble inserting the cannula. This time it took three nurses three attempts before it finally went into a vein in the back of my hand. They took some precautions with a heat pack, and elevated my legs. I used to feel embarrassed with my legs stuck up in the air in the middle of the crowded treatment room, but I was getting used to it now. Thankfully, there was no fainting and they managed to avoid using my 'fainting hand'.

Once again, I occupied my time during the treatment by watching TV on my tablet. This time my brain did go a little funny in as far as I struggled to recall certain words such as 'courgette' at teatime. And my speech became a little slurred for a short time. It reminded me of chemo but the side effects were not as severe, nor did they last as long.

I was extremely drowsy during and after the treatment, which was to be expected. I had a good night's sleep and the following day I felt more like myself.

On 13th March 2017 I blogged:

> It's quite nice to be able to say that life has been rather busy recently (back at work, an eight-week-old daughter, music and church things

picking up) as opposed to being wiped out on the sofa and able to do nothing.

It has been good getting back to 'normal'. Even now I still have to stop and remind myself that I am just coming out the other side of experiencing a big trauma. It still feels as if it has not happened to me and was all somehow a bad dream.

Recovery has been interesting so far. Mentally, all I want to do is get on with things. My mind wants to press on as if nothing has happened, as if my illness has been an inconvenient blip on the landscape of my life that I can now forget about – although I can't forget about it, so instead it acts as a constant reminder that life is short and needs to be lived to the full, right now!

My body has been saying, 'Easy does it. Take things one step at a time. Don't push yourself too hard but do take small steps towards recovering.' After driving in to work for the first few weeks, I can now walk the thirty minutes to get there. The walk does me good and doesn't finish me off. However, I have been accepting lifts back home again at the end of the day. There are some days when I do feel exhausted, so I am still trying to get the balance right.

My spirit is saying, 'Your suffering was not a blip to be forgotten. It is now an essential part of your life. It has helped to form you and to deepen your maturity. Your relationship with God has grown and so have you. Do not dismiss what you have learned through your suffering.'

Three months later, I found myself researching non-Hodgkin lymphoma online on the Lymphoma Association UK website.[29] The things I read, I already knew, such as the type of lymphoma I have cannot be cured; it will come back again, and it will be treated again; people with this type of lymphoma are very likely to live for many years. Although this was supposed to be reassuring, it did not fill me with much joy. I want to live a *good*, long life.

I now felt well. I was no longer nauseous or weak or terribly fatigued. I no longer felt out of my depth and completely out of control. I was no longer blogging about the most recent setback or hospitalisation. I had started to do the things I did before I was diagnosed. By this time, I had returned to my teaching job full-time and ministry opportunities were opening up. I was travelling around the UK about once a month to either sing or speak (and sometimes both). A book[30] I had started writing before I was diagnosed was in its final stages of completion and I was planning a launch event.

As a family, we had begun to plan and to dream again for the future. We had booked a short holiday away during the summer holidays.

I saw all of this as excellent progress.

---

[29] lymphoma-action.org.uk/types-lymphoma/non-hodgkin-lymphoma (accessed 10th June 2021).

[30] Matt McChlery, *All Things New: Stories of Transformed Lives* (Wisbech: Faithseed Books, 2021). Available from Matt McChlery Ministries, www.mattmcchlery.com.

However, in the middle of it all, the illusion of control had very easily and quickly crept back into my mindset to some extent.

When things are going well, we find it comfortable to believe we are in complete control of our lives. We can decide, and plan, and act. We expect things to happen as we want them to. One of the lessons I learned during my time with cancer is that we are not in control. But God is.

I have been caught off guard every now and then, when I can peer through this illusion of control for a moment. When conversation moves to future events, such as my girls starting school or what to do about our pension, I catch a glimpse of the fragility of life. I am reminded that I am not in control, and thoughts like 'I may not be there for this – I pray that by God's grace I will be' swirl around my mind. I am reminded that death is not that far away, and it often reminds me of its presence.

In June 2017, I wrote:

> A couple of days ago I found myself quite sad, beginning to let the thoughts of doubt and 'what ifs' start to cloud my thinking. So I prayed.
>
> I was reminded that I can choose to live in God's peace, just as I did while going through chemotherapy. I realised I needed to accept my feelings of fear and hopelessness – not suppress them and try to ignore them or squeeze them into a corner of my mind. But once acknowledged and accepted, I needed to offer them to God.
>
> I have come to realise that my 'normal' is forever altered. I am indeed living life with faith and

cancer. Yes, I trust and pray with all my heart that God will heal me. However, I am in a strange place of never being able to know if I have been healed or not. Either the cancer will come back, or it won't. I will forever live in a state of hope and faith that I will be healed, but I will not know this for sure until I am in eternity. This is my new normal.

Allowing the illusion of control to enter my thought process will do nothing to help me. I need to continually be reminded that I live by the grace of God. That every single day is a precious gift of life and I get to choose how to live it. I hope I choose to live it well. To make a difference for the good of those who know me and the world around me. I hold this verse close to my heart:

So be careful how you live. Don't live like fools, but like those who are wise. Make the most of every opportunity in these evil days. Don't act thoughtlessly, but understand what the Lord wants you to do.
(Ephesians 5:15-17, NLT)

Only God is in control. None of us knows what will happen next – not really.

I choose to trust, to accept where I am, to surrender my control to the One who is already in control, and know that no matter what happens, 'It is Well with My Soul'.[31]

---

[31] Title of hymn by Horatio Spafford (1828-88).

21
The Aftermath

It had now been more than a year since I had been told I was in remission. Praise God!

However, my family and I were still healing. The emotional and psychological impact of a trauma, such as dealing with a family member living through a time with cancer, continues to persist even when the trauma itself is apparently over.

After a hurricane, there is a mass of debris and destruction left in its wake, with cars upturned and battered, trees ripped out from their roots and flung about like a box of open matches, roofs ripped off houses and buildings smashed. You get the picture.

Shortly after the devastation, a massive clean-up operation usually begins. Most buildings are rebuilt. Trees replanted. Roads remade. However, there are some things that take a long time to be repaired, or indeed are never repaired even many years later. For example, house building was still taking place fourteen years after

Hurricane Katrina made landfall in New Orleans in 2005 in the Lower Ninth Ward of the city.[32]

It takes a long time to deal with some of the effects of a catastrophic event, even when the event itself ended some time ago.

My wife and I had reached a point where my realism had crashed into her optimism.

It was painful and tearful.

I was in remission. She clung on to her belief that God had healed me totally and completely. I fully believed that if God wanted to do this, He could and He would – but He might not. We had to come to a place where we could hold our belief and trust in God and His ability to heal in tension and balance with the possibility that He may not choose to heal me, and that my cancer might return one day.

General illness also pressed some new buttons for us.

I found I now caught viruses, like colds, more easily than I did before the cancer and the chemo. Whenever I got ill, a whole mix of emotions came to the surface in Verity, as well as in me. These included anger – that I was ill again, and she really didn't want to lose me. I got cross with her as I felt she didn't really want to acknowledge that I was ill and didn't show much sympathy, but she was just trying to deal with her emotions and cope with the situation; and fear – that the cancer might return one day. Fear that I would die and leave her and my lovely little girls behind. There was also a fear that we might have to

---

[32] eesi.org/articles/view/fourteen-years-later-new-orleans-is-still-trying-to-recover-from-hurricane-katrina (accessed 16th September 2021).

go through the trauma and treatments and pain all over again. These were just a couple of the effects of the devastation we were navigating at that time.

As we talked things through and prayed about what was going on, things started to get better. Healing came, both emotionally and psychologically. But it took a long while. In fact, I would not be surprised if many years down the line we come across more debris from the storm that we need to deal with. The healing process is not just a physical one, and it takes time.

On 11th April 2018 I blogged:

> Adjusting to living post-cancer can be a challenge in and of itself. I have found I need to find a new 'normal'. I am finding this stage of recovery a bit like walking a tightrope … where I am constantly balancing my 'old' normal with the 'new' normal. Where I can forget all about cancer one minute and then the next minute, I will be navigating thoughts of fear and doubt.
>
> Now that I have been in remission for over a year, cancer is no longer all-consuming, and I am freely able to think about other things. This is fuelled by the ability to do the things I used to do too – go for walks, play guitar, go back to work, do the shopping, look after the kids, etc.
>
> In fact, days and even weeks can go by where I do not think about cancer at all. Life is no longer how it used to be. I am having to adjust to living in a new 'normal'.
>
> There are times when thoughts about cancer do creep up on me. This can be quite sudden and

unexpected. Watching an advert on TV about a cancer charity run or an appeal for fundraising often makes my thoughts return to it, although not in an unpleasant way.

The moments I am having to be careful of are when discussion turns to a subject that involves living longer. For example, talk about reaching a significant birthday (even if it's someone else talking about themselves), discussions about 'when you are a grandparent...' or 'when your girls become teenagers...' These are perfectly normal things to talk about and I am not asking people to avoid these topics when I am around. It's just that I find myself immediately thinking negatively about my life in times like these.

You might have the impression that I am an extremely positive person. I must confess that naturally, I am not. I gravitate towards being quite negative and pessimistic if left to my own devices – just ask my wife. I have found that it is my faith in Jesus that helps me to be more positive and this is what gives me hope.

So it is at those times, when long life is being discussed, I often find myself saying in my head, 'Wouldn't it be great if I reached forty? Getting to sixty would be a bonus!' or, 'I really hope I make it to see my daughters reach their teenage years.' I need to catch myself. I need to choose to think positively again.

Squashing the feelings of fear and doubt somewhere deep inside is not the answer. That only increases the pressure and the pain. I need to remind myself again and again of what Jesus taught me while I was in the middle of the storm: Jesus is in control, not me. All I need to do is trust in Him and rest. That is all. Hold firmly on to Jesus and ride the next wave, wherever it may take me.

Later that month I was having another top-up treatment. It was only when I sat down in the chair that I suddenly remembered that I had forgotten to drink lots of water in the hours leading up to my tenth maintenance treatment. Oh no. Drinking lots of water has, in the past, helped to enlarge my veins a bit and, as a result, helped with the cannula going in. But this was not to be on this occasion – my fault, I know.

The first attempt found a vein in the top of my hand, which is the usual place for my cannula to go. But the flow was not good. This meant that the medicine would struggle to get into my body. So we needed to have another go elsewhere.

This time, a vein was found to the side of my upper wrist. They hadn't gone in this high up before. Wow – this one hurt. The nurse found a good vein that was flowing well. But the pain continued and continued. This was all it took – I felt my stomach begin to churn, my skin went hot and clammy. I felt lightheaded and then I fainted.

The nurses and I always had a laugh after one of my fainting spells, which the nurses were quite used to by now. My reputation for being a 'fainter' was once again confirmed. I joked with one of them that when she saw my name on the treatment list in the morning, she had asked someone else to cannulate me. This caused a lot of laughter because I think it was true.

The rest of the treatment went well. I felt really sleepy as usual and just watched some TV on my tablet.

Usually, my maintenance treatments just left me feeling tired. But this time I felt a bit ill too. Not as poorly as the full chemo made me feel, but I was a little under the weather.

After a good night's sleep, I was feeling much better and was able to return to normal – changing nappies, getting bottles of milk ready for the girls, etc. We even had a barbecue in the afternoon that we invited the family around for.

It was a good day.

22
Ring the Bell

Cancer made me re-evaluate how I was living my life.

For a while, I had been praying and asking God how He wanted me to spend my time and earn my money. At this point I had already been doing increasingly more work for my local church both behind the scenes and up front.

I was trying to write a new book about my experiences of living life with faith and cancer to help others and their families who find themselves in a similar position (which you are holding in your hands right now). However, finding the space and time to do this was extremely difficult.

I had been a primary school teacher for fifteen years, fourteen of which I spent at the same school. It had been a good time of my life. I had learned a lot, as well as taught a lot. However, I had come to the point where I felt as if I was just going through the motions. My work–life balance was constantly being eroded, which saw me leaving home earlier and returning home later each day. This is not how I wanted to spend the rest of my life – this life that we had all fought so hard to keep. The time had come for me to move on.

I was praying and asking God if He wanted me to leave teaching. I needed Him to open a door for me to leave. Past experiences in life (such as applying for the visa to move to the UK) had taught me not to jump ahead of God's plan or timing but rather to wait until He 'gave the nod'. I knew I was going to leave; it was just a matter of waiting for God's timing.

A couple of weeks before the Easter holiday, the staff in our department were called to a meeting where we were told that we were overstaffed for the coming school year, so this meant a redundancy had to be made. The first step of the process was to open it up for a volunteer to come forward to take the redundancy voluntarily. If this did not happen after we got back from the holiday, we would then enter a process where the management would decide who it would be.

I prayed about it. My wife and I discussed it. We also received counsel from a few trusted church leaders with whom we had already been sharing our initial thoughts. It was clear to all of us that this was the sign we had been waiting for. The time for me to leave teaching had arrived.

Without too much hesitation, I took a deep breath and wrote my letter, volunteering for redundancy.

My letter was accepted, and so I began to prepare to leave the school I had been at for more than a third of my life.

People were asking me, 'What will you do? Have you got another job? Are you going to carry on teaching?'

Honestly, my main plan was to trust God. I'd been in this position before, when I decided to emigrate to the UK, and God was faithful then. I was confident that He would not fail me.

I had several ideas of what I could do, but finding out if they lined up with God's ideas was going to be part of the adventure. I hoped to become self-employed and to work full-time in church ministry – the place where my passion and heart was, serving both my local church community as well as other churches further afield with my writing, music and preaching. I also hoped to set up a small private tutoring business, which would enable me to still use my teaching skills.

I had also recently watched a movie[33] that I had found particularly inspiring. The final words summarised quite beautifully some of the thoughts I was having at the time. In essence, it said that taking risks is an important part of what it means to be alive. We need to be brave enough to take risks, to move forward into the future with faith and hope and to celebrate change as it carries us away from where we are towards where we are going.

This film seemed to confirm what I believed I was hearing God telling me to do. To take a risk, to embrace the joy of doing things that I loved. To do the things that God had called me to do. So it seemed to me that this was another source of confirmation that it was right for me to leave my teaching job and to step out in faith.

Despite being in remission from cancer, in some ways it never leaves you. It lurks like an unwanted memory, a

---

[33] *The Best Exotic Marigold Hotel* (2011). Distributed by Fox Seachlight Pictures.

distant shadow from the past clinging on to the present. Every now and then that shadow steps a little closer and makes itself known, bringing with it doubt, worry and fear.

A few days after my maintenance treatment in June 2018, these fears stepped out of the shadows again. Based on my recent experiences I have learned to listen to my body and not to ignore it.

I noticed a discomfort in my lower left back. After doing activity or after being on my feet all day at work, this discomfort could turn to pain. I had no idea what it was, or what was the cause. I went to the GP. They had a look, as I thought it could be a side effect of some medication I had recently been put on for a mild skin condition. They tested my kidney function and had a poke around my abdomen area.

The niggling thought that the general location of the discomfort was exactly where the massive tumour had been located before my chemotherapy saw the shadow step closer.

In the following weeks, the discomfort came and went in slightly diminishing degrees. As it had not resolved itself, I went back to the GP and he referred me to the consultant at the hospital. A CT scan and blood tests were done.

At my regular pre-treatment clinic with my consultant, we discussed the results of the scan and I was relieved to learn that the cancer had not returned. In fact, he told me that the remaining scar tissue had reduced in size since the last time we had a scan done.

Truth is often described as 'light', and now knowing that this discomfort was not cancer, the light of this knowledge caused the shadows of doubt and concern to retreat.

The doctor suggested it could be caused by the scar tissue slowly breaking down. The GP thought it could be something to do with my colon.

This put my mind at ease.

On 11th August 2018 I blogged:

> It seems I have been going through a lot of 'endings' recently but entering into new beginnings at the same time.
>
> A few weeks ago, I left my teaching job of fourteen years.
>
> Yesterday saw another ending occur. I had my final maintenance treatment session at hospital.
>
> When you first hear the word 'cancer' and you feel as though the whole world is caving in around you, it is very hard to look years ahead into the future to the day when you are cancer-free and your treatment ends – and you get to walk away, pick up the pieces and to continue living this beautiful thing called life.
>
> After walking a long road, I can now say that this particular chapter of my life has ended. A recent PET scan showed that the treatment has been successful and I am cancer-free with no trace of lymphoma in my body. Thank the Lord. Yesterday I got to say goodbye to the very dedicated and caring team of chemo nurses at the Queen Elizabeth Hospital in King's Lynn

who have been there every step of the way and have become friends.

As I left the treatment room, as is the tradition for survivors on the day their treatment ends, I rang a special bell which is attached to the wall by the chemo room door. A little silly, some may think, but it is good to celebrate your successes, and surviving cancer certainly is a success. At first, I did feel a little silly ringing the bell, but as I rung it, it occurred to me that I wasn't just ringing the bell for me. I was ringing the bell for everyone else in the room too. Everyone else who was hooked up to their chemo treatments who were travelling on the same journey ... Weathering similar storms to mine.

Hearing the bell being rung from someone at the end of their journey gives hope and determination for those still running the race to continue, to keep going, to keep hoping, to keep praying, to keep on keeping on.

I hope these words bring you some comfort, some hope and stir courage within you as I 'ring my bell' – I hope you can hear it and be encouraged to keep going.

I now close this chapter of my life and take a deep breath as I stretch out my hand in faith, grasp the door handle of opportunity that God has placed in front of me and give it a tug...

21
2021

The year is 2021, and as I glance over my shoulder and look back at my life, the storm that I went through five years ago seems to be a long way in the distance. It was dark and terrifying, but its pain has become dulled by the passage of time. I no longer dream about it at night, nor am I constantly plagued with thoughts about cancer during the day. Things that would trigger panic, such as an advert for a cancer charity on TV, no longer trigger me. Balance and order have returned. Things are different, yet things are good. Living with faith and cancer will forever remain an extremely significant part of my life, and my experiences have given me a story worth sharing, for which I am grateful.

Over the years, as I have told others about my experiences, numerous people have opened up to me about their struggles and trials with cancer. I pray that my hope in Jesus and the sharing of my story can point them towards Him.

As soon as we were able to try for children again after my maintenance treatments had finished, we were blessed with the miracle of another child. Elijah was born in 2019.

He is now a bubbly, friendly and energetic one-and-a-half-year-old boy who loves to run about the place, terrorising his two older sisters, whom he adores.

Since leaving my job in 2018, I can confirm it was the right decision for me. I continue to live each day by faith, trusting that Jesus will provide for my needs. I earn significantly less than I did when I was employed by someone else, but now that I am self-employed my quality of life has increased, and so has my well-being and my joy. I am doing the things I love to do and wake up with a sense of purpose each day.

When people ask me what I do for a living, I warn them that they are about to get a rather complicated answer. Primarily I work for the church. I am now part of the senior leadership team. I preach and teach regularly as well as still play a bit of guitar in the church band. I head up the church communications as well as deal with all the technology such as websites and the church livestream on the internet. I lead the Messy Church, which is a great time of fun and encounter with Jesus for all ages, especially those who are curious about what faith in Jesus is all about. I continue to write songs about faith, and opportunities to perform further afield in other churches, coffee shops and festivals opened up after I left teaching. I have been in a recording studio a few times and have released a number of singles and mini-albums, known in the trade as EPs or 'Extended Play' recordings.

I have been throwing myself more into developing my skills as an author and have been focusing on my writing. I have had a couple of shorter pieces published in a writers' magazine and also in a devotional book. I have updated a revised edition of my very first book[34] that I wrote about the songwriting process and have spent a lot of time working on the book you are now reading. I am also an administrator for a local charity that allocates grants to help alleviate poverty or to improve the education of youngsters in my local town.

I haven't completely abandoned my primary school teacher training as I still put those skills to good use three evenings a week, when I tutor children from within the comfort of my study, which is a garage that we have converted.

One important lesson I have learned is that I am not defined by the job I do or the work I complete. These things are important, but what I do is no longer a big part of my identity. The important thing that defines me is who Jesus says I am and what His Word, the Bible, says about me, and indeed, about all of those who choose to follow Jesus.

I am loved. I am chosen.[35] I am unique and special. I am more than what I do. I am more than what has happened to me. I am not abandoned[36] or forgotten.[37] There are times when life gets difficult, as life always does; then I am reminded of what Jesus has already done for me and of the storms He has already carried me through. If He has been faithful in the past, as He was in 2016, I can be sure

---

[34] Matt McChlery, *Songcraft: Exploring the Art of Christian Songwriting* (Wisbech: Faithseed Books, 2021). Available from Matt McChlery Ministries, www.mattmcchlery.com.

[35] John 15:16.

[36] Deuteronomy 31:6.

[37] Psalm 115:12.

that He will continue to be faithful in the storms that lie ahead.

My faith in Jesus continues to carry me through life. He is the greatest friend I could ever have. My life is built upon His solid and firm foundation, upon the Rock that does not change.[38] He was the One who held me close when the storms came crashing in and He will be the One who will hold me again in the storms to come. And one day, when my journey is done, He will be the One who holds me even closer as He carries me home.

---

[38] Malachi 3:6.

Author's Thanks

Living in the UK and being a British citizen meant I was fortunate enough to benefit from the amazing NHS. This meant that all my healthcare costs were paid for by the state. I received all my treatments and medications, hospital admissions and more besides, free. I was also paid statutory sick pay by the school which meant our bills were paid throughout my time of treatment and recovery. I am aware that if I had still been in Zimbabwe there would be no way that my medical aid insurance would have covered my treatment, and the outcome could have sadly been very different. Many people complain about the NHS, but I have found it to be truly amazing and it has quite literally saved my life.

I would like to thank...

The NHS doctors, staff and Macmillan nurses at the Queen Elizabeth Hospital in King's Lynn, Norfolk, for all they have done for me.

My darling wife, who has truly stuck by my side in sickness and in health.

My children, Katrina, Lara and Elijah – you are precious, and you are loved. I am so grateful that I get to be part of your lives.

Claris Tan in the Philippines, as well as the numerous others around the world, both friends and strangers, who have shared this journey with me and who were praying for me throughout 2016.

Nicki Copeland and the team at Instant Apostle, for taking a risk on me by publishing this book.

Everyone in the Brecks, Fens and Pens writers' group, for your tireless encouragement, advice and friendship.

The Association of Christian Writers (ACW) who have helped me to navigate the publishing world.

My amazing church family at The King's Church, Wisbech – thank you for your love and support.

Reliable Cancer Websites

The internet is awash with websites offering information, advice and cures for cancer. I have seen many, and to be honest, some are very suspicious. All along I have gone with the belief that God can heal me, but He has also given gifts and talents of varying kinds to human beings, including intellect and scientific understanding. He may be choosing to heal me through the skill, research and medicines that have been developed.

I have tried to include in this list websites that provide trustworthy and credible information about cancer as well as those charities who work to help those with the disease.

CANCER RESEARCH
www.cancerresearchuk.org

CHILDREN WITH CANCER UK
www.childrenwithcancer.org.uk

LYMPHOMA ACTION
www.lymphoma-action.org.uk

MACMILLAN CANCER SUPPORT
www.macmillan.org.uk

MARIE CURIE – Terminal Illness Support
www.mariecurie.org.uk

NHS
www.nhs.uk/conditions/cancer/

TEENAGE CANCER TRUST
www.teenagecancertrust.org

YOUNG LIVES vs CANCER[39]
www.younglivesvscancer.org.uk

---

[39] Formerly CLIC Sargent.